JUSTICE

Military Tribunals in Civil War Missouri

J. B. King

RED ENGINE PRESS

Library of Congress Control Number: 2017931899

Paperback ISBN: 978-1-943267-32-3
ebook ISBN: 978-1-943267-33-0

Front Cover Art by Ken Miller - "Union soldiers in disguise attempt to rob a homeowner near Rolla."

Back Cover Art & Inside Illustrations by Robyn Cook

Printed in the United States.

Red Engine Press

Dedication

This book is dedicated to the two people who really count in my life: My wife Cheryl, and my son Taylor. Without you my life would be very lonely. Thanks for putting up with me before and after I worked on this book. The two of you are the light of my life, and you make the world a good place to live.

TABLE OF CONTENTS

Introduction

As the years passed after the publication of my first book, *The Tilley Treasure*, I found myself in a position that I can best describe as a big history frog in a medium-sized pond. And I kept getting the same question: when are you going to write another book? The answer was simple, job pressure made that impossible. Then in July of 2001, after thirty-two years as a member of the Missouri State Highway Patrol, I was able to retire. And I began to get even more requests for a new book.

The answer was then: yes, I did have the time to write a new book. And, even better, I had an old topic that was still on my mind. For my first book I had obtained copies of trial transcripts on Wilson Tilley and Emily Weaver. These are the types of old history that I like to chase; an unknown story about an unknown person in our history. I had used the Tilley story, but the Weaver story was still untold. I also had another unknown story that was set in Rolla, Missouri I decided it was time to write.

As I completed more research into these cases, I soon found many more cases of military justice which took place here in Missouri. I changed my focus and decided to create a book based on a series of Union Army wartime trials. Sometime in the future I'll know whether or not I made a wise decision.

Over the years I'd listened to a lot of people who had expressed their opinions or complaints about my first book. Actually, the lack of complaints was quite a surprise to me. About the only complaint I did get with any frequency was that my first book was too hard to read. The print size was way too small for a lot of people. Now that I'm older, I seem to have the same problem. But you shouldn't have that problem with this book.

Writing books on history is my hobby. The money that comes in from book sales doesn't pay my rent or buy my food. Every cent I earn goes right back into the history business for more research, expenses, and printing costs. When you buy my history book, you're helping me promote history. I thank you for your support.

During the trials which follow, you may find many strange words about the Civil War. The folks back then had a way of talking and writing that might sound a bit odd to us today. They also used quite a few word-terms that many people won't understand, especially military terms. In order to help in your understanding of the events, I've inserted a series of author's notes into the stories to better explain. In a few places, I've added extra material to give the reader a better sense of Civil War history.

I found myself with a big problem of how to handle some of the trial material, since much of it was of a very boring and repetitive nature. When you read an entire trial transcript you get a whole sense of the story. Many of the words and phrases used by some of the witnesses speak volumes as to conditions of the time. If you leave out some of the material, you lose a lot of history. I had to struggle with a few decisions on just how to handle parts of the material I wanted to present. I've tried to vary my approach with these stories and keep the project interesting. My objective was to always entertain the reader with the enjoyment of history.

I'd like to thank the following people who had a role to play in the creation of this book. I'll start with the staff at the Bruce G. Clarke Library, Ft. Leonard Wood, Missouri. They have two sets of *The War of The Rebellion, Official Records*. When I started my research, book No. 114 was like new. I didn't wear out their copy of book No. 114, but it did get a severe workout. I can only hope I wasn't a pain in their side while I did my research. My wife, Cheryl, was extremely helpful in reading the handwritten scribbles we found on some of the trial transcripts. She works in the medical field and the scribbles were normal writing for her. She also helped me with the typing of the manuscript. Marianne Ward edited the book for mistakes in grammar and English. She found quite a few of them, and the book will flow much more smoothly due to her efforts.

For the book illustrations, and the front and back cover of the book I'd like to thank Robyn Cook and Ken Miller. I learned much from them as we tried to recreate history to fit inside a book. My manuscript printer, Tim Berrier at Lone Oak Printing Company was a very patient fellow who passed along many good ideas that I used in the book. I learned one of life's little lessons many years ago that if you don't know what you're doing, you go to the people who do know how to do it, and you listen carefully to their advice. During my work on this book I found these people qualified to be the experts I needed.

I can share the credit, but the mistakes are all mine. I've printed my permanent mailing address below. If you have a comment about the book, please feel free to write and express your opinion. Likewise, if you have a question please ask, and I'll try to answer all requests for information.

Best wishes and enjoy history,
James B. King, Jr.
P.O. Box 226
Waynesville, MO 65583

Chapter 1

The Bitter Civil War in Missouri

The American Civil War was a bitter time for many people. Those who view the war as a time of gallant actions and deeds need to study more history. Prisoners, combatants, and civilians were murdered or abused by both sides. Rotten prisoner of war camps abounded with poor living conditions. Refugee camps came into existence. Crime was abundant throughout the land. Political abuse toward the people on the opposing side was frequent, with many gross violations of what we would today call human rights. Some of these human rights violations committed by Americans against Americans can only be described as shocking. Photographs taken of prisoners who had been held for long periods of time in Civil War prison camps look exactly the same as the walking skeletons that came out of the German concentration camps of World War II. There are many aspects of our Civil War that should create a sense of national shame in our hearts.

The Civil War here in Missouri was in the same shape or even worse than on the national scene. After all, Missouri was a border state and the clash of views was much more unpredictable. In 1861, if you had sampled the views of one thousand people in South Carolina, the clear majority would have voted Confederate States of America (C.S.A.). If you had gone to Ohio for one thousand people, the vote would have been Union. Here in Missouri it was much more complex.

In 1861, the elected Missouri Governor was Clairborne Fox Jackson, and he promised the Confederacy that Missouri would furnish the southern army with one hundred thousand men. Jackson, however, was out of touch with his people. In fact, Missouri gave the Union one hundred thousand men during the war, and gave the South only forty thousand men. But there was a very clear line of division in the state. The St. Louis area was pro-Union and the rest of the state was pro-Confederate. This general statement oversimplifies the state's position. After all, there were pockets of southern loyalists in St. Louis and Union supporters everywhere in the state, but in the overall picture, there was a clear geographic division between the sides here in Missouri.

The problem in Missouri was also made much more complex when the U.S. Army seized control of the capital in Jefferson City, Missouri. The U.S. Army installed a provisional Governor and a Missouri legislature to govern the state. At the same time, the established Missouri Governor and his loyal southern-view legislative body were forced out of the state in a series of military clashes. The freely elected pre-war Missouri governing body spent the war outside the boundary lines of Missouri. And yes, they passed all kinds of laws and took other kinds of governing actions to run the state. And yes, mass confusion was the order of the day. Whose laws do you obey? To whom do you pay taxes? Whose money do you use to pay the taxes? To whom do you appeal if your family becomes the victim of a crime? If you can't possess a firearm, how do you defend your family? Will the authorities in charge come to your defense? Who is in charge?

In most history books Missouri has been listed as a border state. Front-line state would be more accurate. When you added the lack of law enforcement and the breakup of the local civil government to the mix, the result was disaster. Missouri became a place where each man had to care for himself and his family against the entire country. And, into this world came the army of occupation — the United States Army.

The United States military forces soon found that history does repeat itself. As countless armies in past centuries had found through bitter experience, the rule of war was simple: if you occupy the land, then you must govern the land. And to govern also means to control the lawful order of society. In order to prevent any civil unrest or disobedience against your army, you must control illegal activity.

But many of the local criminal court units were in disorder, and not all of them could function. What do you do to control this problem?

Again, you turn to the past military history of the world and you establish the military commission, or military tribunal. In short, the military becomes the prosecution, the judge, the jury, and executioner. Civil and criminal unrest can then be handled in a halfway-civilized fashion. The bottom line was simple, if you were accused of a disloyal act or crime of some sort you found yourself standing in front of seven or so Union Army officers who decide your fate. What could be more fair?

Fair or unfair, it didn't matter. The military legal rule became the order of the day. But, there was another problem. Some sections of the Missouri Courts *did* continue to function, so not all cases went in front of the military. Some cases were tried by the pre-war legal system. How do you decide which cases go to which legal system? [As I write these words late in the year of 2003, I'm struck by the fact that many of these Civil War arguments over jurisdiction are again in the news with regard to the war on terror. Which terrorists should go to a military tribunal and which to the federal court system?] Action had to be taken; the rule of law was part of the national soul.

Since the dawn of time, all human societies have had some concept of the idea of rule of law. It doesn't matter if we're talking about the United States of America with its two hundred thirty million people, or some remote tribe of two hundred thirty people hidden in the Amazon rainforest. Some type of rule of law applies to the way humans live, work, and die.

The law concept that works in the Amazon may not work well in the United States. The concept of law in the United States has developed into a very complex and formal system. It has a high degree of fixed structure. Most of us have some idea as to the working of the criminal justice system in our world, but the level of justice found during the Civil War world over one hundred fifty years ago was not the same as today. In order to understand just how a Civil War military trial worked, we need to explore the world of trials — modern civil and military-based courts.

As an example from our modern world we can use the idea of ten gang members on a street corner in St. Louis, Missouri. Suddenly, ten rival gang members are on the opposite side of the street. In a case like this, in order to protect their turf, bullets have been known to fly back and forth across the street on very short notice. The police are called and arrive on scene. Some of the gang members are arrested. They could be charged with a wide variety of crimes such as murder, assault, armed criminal action, or possession of an illegal weapon.

The suspects in custody are all given legal counsel and introduced into a fixed judicial system. The term 'fixed judicial system' means the judge and the court system were already in place before the shootout took place. They simply wait for the next group of defendants to appear. Once the defendants appear, each defendant must be advised of the specific charge or charges that are applied to him at his arraignment. In this case, an example might be, "the defendant John Doe did shoot to death George Wilson by means of a dangerous and deadly weapon; a Smith and Wesson 9mm pistol." Following the first appearance and the reading of the charges, the defendant would be required to appear at a preliminary hearing to determine if the charges brought against him have merit and are worth the time of the court system to seek a final determination of the charges. Once the preliminary hearing has been completed, a judge must rule on the case. The judge must decide if a crime was committed, and if the defendant was the probable person who committed that crime. If the answer to both questions is yes, the defendant is bound over to a higher judicial level for a final trial to determine guilt.

The defendant has a very large number of options he can exercise in his defense. He can ask for the judge to be removed, a change of venue to another court, a change of counsel, suppression of the evidence, and a host of other motions. The defendant has the right to go free on bond while he waits for trial. He has the right to a jury trial, where he can face and hear the witnesses against him in open court.

If convicted of a crime, he has the right to appeal his case to a higher level of the judicial system. These appellant courts are composed of judges who have a high level of legal training. During an appeal, these judges only look at the case to determine if the proper law and proceedings were applied during the trial. The appeal process can go through several layers until "the buck stops here." This usually means the Supreme Court of the state in question. However, if a question of federal law can be raised in the case, then it could be transferred to the Federal Court system and move upward through the federal system until it reaches the United States Supreme Court. Sooner or later, usually much later, the case has runs its course and the defendant gets his punishment. Cases that involve the death penalty seem to drag on forever. A defendant may spend ten to twenty years in prison waiting for a death sentence to be imposed.

The military trials of the Civil War operated under a very different system. The system was not fixed in nature and many variations of the same basic system were used. In general, the military commission or Military Tribunal referred to the trial of a civilian violator, or an enemy of the state. The term 'military court-martial' was used when members of your own army committed crimes. Just how did a military court receive the authority to try a civilian? Exactly what were the thoughts of the military men who suddenly found they had to act to preserve law and order in the state? What acts should they take to keep order? Exactly what kind of violations were they worried about? In the mass confusion that ruled during 1861, the Union forces published a number of statements and proclamations to inform the citizens of Missouri of their desire to keep law and order. One of the first was by the Commanding Officer of the Department of Missouri, General John C. Fremont.

> *PROCLAMATION.*
> *HEADQUARTERS WESTERN DEPARTMENT,*
> *Saint Louis, August 30, 1861.*
> *Circumstances in my judgment are of sufficient urgency to render it necessary that the commanding general of this department should assume the administrative powers of the State. Its disorganized condition, helplessness of civil authority, and the total insecurity of life and devastation of property by bands of murderers and marauders who infest*

nearly every county in the State and avail themselves of public misfortunes in the vicinity of a hostile force to gratify private and neighborhood vengeance and who find an enemy wherever they find plunder finally demand the severest measures to repress the daily increasing crimes and outrages which are driving off the inhabitants and ruining the State.

In this condition the public safety and success of our arms require unity of purpose without let or hindrance to the prompt administration of affairs. In order therefore to suppress disorders, maintain the public peace and give security to the persons and property of loyal citizens I do hereby extend and declare established martial law throughout the State of Missouri. The lines of the army occupation in this State are for the present declared to extend from Leavenworth by way of posts of Jefferson City, Rolla and Ironton to Cape Girardeau on the Mississippi River. All persons who shall be taken with arms in their hands within these lines shall be tried by court-martial and if found guilty will be shot. Real and personal property of those who shall take up arms against the United States or who shall be directly proven to have taken an active part with their enemies in the field is declared confiscated to public use and their slaves if any they have are hereby declared free men.

All persons who shall be proven to have destroyed after the publication of this order railroad tracks, bridges or telegraph lines shall suffer the extreme penalty of the law. All persons engaged in treasonable correspondence, in giving or procuring aid to the enemy, in fermenting turmoil and disturbing public tranquility by creating or circulating false reports or incendiary documents are warned that they are exposing themselves.

All persons who have been led away from allegiance are required to return to their homes forthwith. Any such absence without sufficient cause will be held to be presumptive evidence against them.

The object of this declaration is to place in the hands of military authorities power to give instantaneous effect to the existing laws and supply such deficiencies as the conditions of the war demand, but it is not intended to suspend the ordinary tribunals of the country where law will be administered by civil officers in the usual manner and with their customary authority while the same can be peaceably administered.

The commanding general will labor vigilantly for the public welfare and by his efforts for their safety hopes to obtain not only acquiescence but also active support of the people of the country.

J. C. FREMONT

A good deal of political uproar followed General Fremont's proclamation. People throughout Missouri and Washington D.C. could not believe that Fremont had actually written parts of his proclamation. One of those people was President Abraham Lincoln, who sent a special dispatch to Fremont on Sept. 2, 1861. Lincoln revoked Fremont's order to shoot people found with arms. Shortly after this, Lincoln also revoked Fremont's emancipation policy toward the Missouri slaves. Before the year was over, Fremont was revoked as Commanding General and the new Commanding General of the Department of Missouri was appointed; Major General Henry W. Halleck. MG Halleck immediately sent out his own thoughts in the form of General Orders No. 32.

GENERAL ORDERS No. 32.
HEADQUARTERS DEPARTMENT MISSOURI
Saint Louis, Missouri, December 22, 1861.

I. Insurgent rebels scattered through the northern counties of this State, which are occupied by our troops under the guise of peaceful citizens, have resumed their occupation of burning bridges and destroying railroads and telegraph wires. These men are guilty of the highest crime known to the code of war and the punishment is death. Anyone caught in the act will be immediately shot, and any one accused of this crime will be arrested and placed in close confinement until his case can be examined by a military commission and if found guilty he also will suffer death.

II. Where injuries are done to railroads or telegraph lines the commanding officer of the nearest post will immediately impress into service for repairing damages the slaves of all secessionists in the vicinity and if necessary the secessionists themselves and their property. Any pretended Union man having information of intended attempts to destroy such roads and lines or of the guilty parties who does not communicate such intention to the proper authorities and give aid and assistance in arresting and punishing them will be regarded as particeps criminis and treated accordingly.

III. Hereafter the towns and counties in which such destruction of public property takes place will be made to pay the expenses of all repairs unless it be shown that the people of such towns or counties could not have prevented it on account of the superior force of the enemy.

By order of Major General Halleck:
J. C. KELTON,
Assistant Adjutant General

MG Halleck received some help with the formation of his thoughts. With disaster looming throughout the state, help had come from the very top of the government in the form of a Presidential decree from Abraham Lincoln. Lincoln recognized the fact that the United States Constitution was faced with the greatest challenge in history. This was a conflict that could tear the country apart forever. In order to save the Union, drastic action would be required. Lincoln's order was short and to the point. The order concerned the legal term *writ of habeas corpus* and a declaration of martial law. The writ of habeas corpus was usually interpreted to mean bring the defendant who has been detained for a crime before the correct court of jurisdiction. The term comes from Latin and literally means, "You may have the body." Martial law simply meant the military was completely in charge of law and order.

Major General Henry W. Halleck
Commanding in the Department of Missouri
GENERAL: As an insurrection exists in the United States and is in arms in the State of Missouri, you are hereby authorized and empowered to suspend the writ of habeas corpus within the limits of the military division under your command and to exercise martial law as you find it necessary in your discretion to secure the public safety and the authority of the United States. In witness whereof I have hereunto set my hand and caused the Seal of the United States to be affixed at Washington, this 2nd day of December, A.D. 1861.
ABRAHAM LINCOLN
By the President: Wm. H. SEWARD
Secretary of State

The concept of marital law or trial by military commission as it existed in the Civil War would not be familiar to us today. If a man is charged with murder or robbery, we understand these charges. But an army, as a society, exists to kill their enemy to defend the parent society. Therefore, the soldier who kills in battle receives honors. The coward who fails to advance on the enemy, or who refuses to obey a lawful order can find himself in big trouble. Since an army must also be ready to do battle at all times, it must maintain the available pool of manpower. Thus, the man who deserts in the face of the enemy, or the man who falls asleep at his sentry post can also face a court-martial.

These concepts can prove confusing to a civilian, but to a soldier the idea of a sentry asleep at his post means the entire military unit could be in grave danger from a surprise enemy attack. Thus, the idea of a death sentence for the sleeping sentry might be considered a reasonable punishment.

But there were also lesser charges brought in the Civil War. An example of such a case is the *United States v. Pvt. Matthew O. Hare*. It seems that on or about September 6, 1861, Pvt. Hare had some serious problems with his company commander in Rolla, Missouri.

In fact, as you read the charges you might get the idea that Pvt. Hare did not have the proper military attitude in the first place.

The first charge was listed as "breaking through guard lines and leaving camp without leave." The second charge was more serious: "kicking his commanding officer and did threaten to blow up the captain's tent, and various other disrespectful acts." After a very short trial, the eight-man, officer, court-martial board decided Pvt. Hare was guilty on all counts. The punishment was set as having all of the hair on one side of his head shaved off. Pvt. Hare also lost all military pay due to him, and was ordered drummed out of the camp.

On September 9, 1861, the entire regiment was in formation as Pvt. Hare was marched to the center of the ranks. The sentence was then read to the guilty man and the regiment. Hare was then marched to the front gate and thrown out of camp. It would probably be safe to say that Hare did not miss military life and just might have been a happy man out of uniform.

Most people would consider the legal action against Hare as strange and unusual, and they would be correct in their thoughts. But the military trial was different. In order to understand those differences, we will examine a military case. Our example will be a real case: *United States v. W. L. Tilley*.

On June 20,1864, Wilson Leroy Tilley and his companion, Miss Emily Weaver of Batesville, Arkansas were arrested by Union Army counter-intelligence officers near St. Louis, Missouri. The Union Army thought they were spies.

In the civilian world, the judge waits for the next defendant. In the military world, the judge and court must be created by special order for such cases. Thus, the first step in the Tilley trial was the appointment by the Commanding Officer of the Department of Missouri of a trial board to meet and hear the charges against Tilley. The actual trial commission was composed of six Union Army officers; two generals, two colonels, and two captains who were introduced by name and rank.

Since Tilley had no objections to the commissions members, the Commission was then duly sworn by the Judge Advocate, and the

Judge Advocate was duly sworn by the President of the Commission respectively in the presence of the prisoner.

The second formal action was the reading of the charges against Tilley:

Charge First: Violation of the Oath of Allegiance. Specification, In this, that he, W. L. Tilley, citizen of Missouri did, on or about the [date not given] day of August, 1862, take and subscribe an oath before an officer qualified to administer the same, whereby he bound himself to bear true allegiance to the United States, and to support and sustain the Constitution and laws thereof, and afterward, on or about the twenty-fifth day of October, 1863, in the state of Missouri, violated said oath by joining and consorting and acting with enemies of the United States, at war therewith.

Charge second: Being a guerrilla-marauder. Specification, In this, that he, W. L. Tilley, citizen of Missouri did, on or about the twenty-fifth day of October, 1863, unite, consort, and act with rebel enemies of the United States, being military insurgents, bushwhackers and guerrilla-marauders, engaged in marauding and petty warfare against the United States.

The third formal action occurred when W. L. Tilley entered a not guilty plea to all of the charges and specifications before the commission. The United States government then had to prove their case in the most direct fashion possible. The government presented a large number of witnesses to prove the violation. Much of the testimony was of a repeat nature about the same incident. The star witness was Lieutenant Charles C. Twyford, Co. H, 5th Missouri State Militia, who was stationed at Waynesville, Missouri.

LT Twyford was sworn as a witness and testified that on October 25th, 1863, he was ordered to carry out a cavalry patrol southwest from Camp Waynesville to search for a missing local citizen. Fourteen enlisted cavalry troopers accompanied Twyford on the patrol.

The first day was quiet, and the patrol camped that night at a location some fourteen miles from the fort. At approximately 0300 hours on the morning of October 26,1863, the night sentry alerted the unit to the fact that unknown persons were approaching the camp. The Union unit went on full alert. The men were then fired upon from the woods, and the rifle fire wounded one Union soldier. At dawn the threat was gone, so LT Twyford sent the wounded man back to camp with an escort of seven troopers. Twyford and six troopers continued the patrol.

Sometime near noon on October 26,1863, Twyford and his men stopped for a meal at the cabin of Hiram King. While eating, they were surprised by the sudden charge of some seventy-five bushwhackers and one hundred fifty regular Confederate troops. The Union soldiers took cover in the cabin and opened fire on the enemy. LT Twyford and his men were able to hold off the enemy for about three hours. When the enemy managed to set the cabin on fire, the Union soldiers had the choice of surrender or death by fire. They decided their best course was surrender.

In his official report of the events, Twyford wrote:

> *We burned all of the papers that would give any of our names or identify us in any way, changed our names, company and regiment for the reason that the bushwhackers had often sworn and circulated the report in the county that if Frank Mason, Michael Williams, and Lieutenant Twyford should fall into their hands, they would burn of shoot them full of holes. We thought it best to assume fictitious names.*

LT Twyford and his men surrendered to Confederate Colonel Love. The bushwhackers made some severe threats toward the Union prisoners and COL Love had to act. COL Love had accepted the Union soldiers surrender and had given his word that they would be treated with honor. He tried several ways to control the situation to prevent the bushwhackers from killing the prisoners. In the end, COL Love was forced to have his regular troops hold the bushwhackers at gunpoint and he sent the prisoners toward Lebanon, Missouri, under the guard of other regular troops. When they were close to the Union Army camp at Lebanon, the prisoners were released on their parole and walked into the camp as free men [Author's note: parole was a word of honor system that required the paroled man to leave the war and not take any further part in war action.]

Due to COL Love's concern and effort, LT Twyford and his men survived the patrol and as a result on February 10,1865, Twyford was the first man to testify at the trial of W. L. Tilley. Twyford described Tilley's role in the fight in great detail, and even named Tilley as one of the leaders of the bushwhackers.

After many other witnesses appeared the trial was concluded. The fourth formal action of the Commission was the verdict. The verdict in this case was hardly a surprise to anyone, the commission found Tilley guilty on all counts.

The Commission then went to the fifth formal action of the trial. The sentence was as follows:

> *And the Commission does therefore sentence him, W. L. Tilley, to imprisonment during the war, at such place as the General commanding the department shall designate.*

The finding of the Commission was confirmed and W. L. Tilley was turned over to the Provost Marshal General. Tilley spent the rest of the war in the Union Army prison at Alton, Illinois.

In Tilley's case, the sixth formal action, an appeal, did not occur. Tilley didn't appeal his case to a higher military authority. In many cases, and in most death penalty cases, the case was sent up the military chain of command for review and approval. Almost all death penalty cases went to the United States Judge Advocate General, Joseph Holt. In many of these cases, Holt himself went to a higher authority. The case stopped at the desk of Abraham Lincoln. Lincoln had the final word on each case, including the six cases featured in this book. Lincoln was an extremely busy man who had a country to run and a war to supervise. But despite that fact, he also took the time to review many military trial cases. The mental strain of deciding which man should be punished or which man should die had to be particularly stressful.

With the end of 1861, the fighting in the east increased and as the war moved into 1862 the Union began to suffer severe losses of life in combat. As the war intensified so did the attitude toward the criminal element, or those people who had committed disloyal acts against the federal government. In early 1862, another Union Army decree was published on the subject of law and order violations.

> *GENERAL ORDERS No. 17.*
> *HEADQUARTERS DISTRICT CENTRAL MISSOURI,*
> *Jefferson City, Mo., April 22, 1862.*
>
> *I. It is with feelings of unfeigned horror at the hellish crimes perpetrated and a profound loathing, abhorrence and disgust for the fiendish outlaws who committed them that the brigadier-general commanding the District of Central Missouri once more calls the attention of the U.S. troops both volunteer and Missouri State Militia under his command to the necessity of increased and constant vigilance tempered with caution and prudence as well as justice and protection toward the innocent, in order that these great, growing and terrible outrages of every sort may be put an end to and the outlaws infesting the district exterminated.*
>
> *Reports of murders, robberies and indeed of every crime known as felony and less criminal offenses reach these headquarters from every part of the district so that it has become dangerous for peaceful, law-abiding citizens and especially good Union citizens to pursue their legitimate vocation without molestation and imminent danger. The country is infested with bands of murderers, robbers and other outlaws of every shade of turpitude known to the criminal calendar, and in some instances (as recent evidence too plainly proves) these wretches are disguised under the uniform of our patriotic army and are pretending to act under and by authority of the United States. These base and bloodthirsty beasts in human form have by their deeds; their boasts and their threats placed themselves beyond the pale of law and must be dealt with accordingly. As the innocent victims of these miscreants are made to suffer without cause and without trial or hearing of any sort (save their cries for mercy uttered in the agonies of terror and death which pass unheeded) so must their brutal,*

lawless and vandal tormentors be dealt with and no mercy shown them. Reasoning with outlaws is of no avail. The law and its faithful officers are set at defiance by these armed and ruthless agents of anarchy and hence they must be subjected to their own code and punished without mercy upon the spot when found enacting or banded together for the enactment of their foul deeds. It is therefore ordered for the observance of all concerned:

II. That hereafter whenever and wherever bands of guerrillas, jayhawkers, marauders, murderers, & etc., are found in arms in open opposition to the laws and legitimate authorities of the United States and the State of Missouri the miscreants of which they are composed are to be shot down by the military authorities when commanded by commissioned officers upon the spot where caught perpetrating their foul acts. And at all times and in all places when our troops no matter by whom commanded are forcibly opposed by outlaws these latter are to be exterminated at all hazards.

III. That all persons who have or shall in future knowingly harbor or in any manner encourage guerrillas, jayhawkers, robbers, murderers or other outlaws in their nefarious deeds will be arrested and kept in close confinement until tried by a military commission or other court as may be deemed expedient at the time.

IV. That where evidence cannot be produced to establish the guilt of parties accused of harboring and encouraging the lawless marauders, & etc., above named but against whom there is strong circumstantial evidence and suspicion they are to be placed under heavy bonds with good and reliable security to keep the peace and for their future good conduct and also required to take the oath of allegiance; and when they refuse or neglect to do this they are to be confined and so held until released by proper authority.

By order of Brig Gen James Totten, Commanding District:
LUCIEN J. BARNES,

Captain and Assistant Adjutant General.

As the war between the United States and the Confederate States entered into the second year of the conflict, the stage was set for more trouble. There would be many more military trials in 1862. These would be more polished than some of the hasty trials that had occurred in 1861.

Within the pages of this chapter you have read a lot of bitter, hateful, or stern comments made by Union Army officers about suspected southern people, disloyal acts, and a host of other topics. Since this was a Civil War which divided the people of our nation, these types of remarks were not exactly one-sided in nature. The following selections don't pertain to the premise of this book but are included to provide you with a more useful understanding of the Civil War, and to increase your knowledge of history. The following southern proclamations share their view of the war.

PROCLAMATION.
JEFFERSON CITY, August 20, 1861.
To THE PEOPLE OF MISSOURI:

FELLOW CITIZENS: The army under my command has been organized under the laws of the State for the protection of your homes and firesides and for the maintenance of the rights, dignity and honor of Missouri.

It is kept in the field for these purposes alone, and to aid in accomplishing them our gallant Southern brethren have come into our State with these. We have achieved a glorious victory over the foe, and scattered far and wide the well-appointed army which the usurper at Washington has been more than six months gathering for your subjugation and enslavement.

This victory frees a large portion of the State from the powers of the invaders and restores it to the protection of its army. It consequently becomes my duty to assure you that it is my firm determination to protect every peaceable citizen in the full enjoyment of all his right whatever may have been his sympathies in the present unhappy struggle, if he has not taken an active part in the cruel warfare which has been waged against the good people of this State by the ruthless enemies whom we have just defeated.

I therefore invite all good citizens to return to their homes and the practice of their ordinary avocations with the full assurance that they, their families, their homes and their property shall be carefully protected. I at the same time warn all evil-disposed persons who may support the usurpations of any one claiming to be provisional or temporary governor of Missouri or who shall in any other way give aid or comfort to the enemy that they will be held as enemies and treated accordingly.

STERLING PRICE,

Major General, Commanding Missouri State Guard.

PROCLAMATION

HDQRS. 1ST MILITARY DIST., MO. STATE GUARD,

Camp Hunter, September 2, 1861.

TO WHOM IT MAY CONCERN:

Whereas, Maj. Gen. John C. Fremont, commanding the minions of Abraham Lincoln in the State of Missouri, has seen fit to declare martial law throughout the whole State and has threatened to shoot any citizen soldier found in arms within certain limits, also to confiscate the property and free the Negroes belonging to the members of the Missouri State Guard: therefore, know ye that I, M. Jeff. Thompson, Brigadier General of the First Military District of Missouri, having not only the military authority of brigadier-general but certain police powers granted by Acting Governor Thomas C. Reynolds and confirmed afterward by Governor Jackson do most solemnly promise that for every member of the Missouri State Guard or soldier of our allies the armies of the Confederate States who shall be put to death in pursuance of said order of General Fremont I will hang, draw and quarter a minion of said Abraham Lincoln.

While I am anxious that this unfortunate war shall be conducted if possible upon the most liberal principles of civilized warfare and every order that I have issued has been with that object yet if this rule is to be adopted (and it must first be done by our enemies) I intend to exceed General Fremont in his excesses and will make all Tories that come in my reach rue the day that a different policy was adopted by their leaders. Already mills, barns, warehouses and other private property have been wastefully and wantonly destroyed by the enemy in this district while we have taken nothing except articles strictly contraband or absolutely necessary. Should these things be repeated I will retaliate ten-fold, so help me God.

M. JEFF. THOMPSON,

Brigadier General, First Military District of Missouri.

Chapter 2

Early Missouri Trials

During the first few months of the war there were a number of arrests in Missouri for various violations. Many of these went before military commissions for trial. Since this was the early part of the war, when it came to the trials there was some confusion on the part of the army about the procedure of how to conduct a trial. Exactly what should you do with some of these defendants? How should you proceed? What if someone made a horrible mistake? And mistakes were made, as the following military correspondence illustrates.

> *SAINT LOUIS, December 31, 1861.*
>
> *Brigadier General POPE, Otterville.*
>
> *GENERAL: I send herewith the proceedings of a military commission ordered by Colonel Deitzler, First Kansas Regiment, for the trial of certain prisoners at Tipton, Mo., within the limits of your command.*
>
> *In the first place, a military commission can be ordered only by the General-in-Chief of the Army or by a general commanding a department, consequently all the proceedings of the commission ordered by Colonel Deitzler are null and void. The prisoners are therefore in precisely the same position as if no trial had taken place.*
>
> *In the second place, military commissions should as a general rule be resorted to only for cases, which cannot be tried by a court-martial or by a proper civil tribunal. They are in other words tribunals of necessity, organized for the investigation and punishment of offenses, which would otherwise*

go unpunished. Their proceedings should be regulated by the rules governing courts-martial so far as they may be applicable and the evidence should in all cases be fully recorded.

Prisoners of war, properly so-called — that is men duly enrolled and commissioned in the service of an acknowledged enemy — are so far as the military authorities are concerned to be treated in the manner prescribed by the usages and customs of war. They are entitled to the rights of war but this fact does not exempt them from punishment by the civil tribunals for treason to the Government. But treason is an offense technically defined by the Constitution and is not triable by a military commission; nor will such tribunal try or punish a soldier duly enrolled and mustered into the enemy's service by proper authority for taking life in battle or according to the rules of modern warfare. But it is a well-established principle that insurgents and marauding, predatory and guerrilla bands are not entitled to this exemption. Such men are by the laws of war neither regarded as no more nor less than murderers, robbers and thieves. The military garb and name cannot change the character of their offenses nor exempt them from punishment. Moreover, if a prisoner of war has committed acts in violation of the laws of war such as murder, robbery, arson, & etc., the fact of his being a prisoner of war does not exempt him from trial and punishment by a military commission. In such cases the charge should be violation of the laws of war, and not violation of the Rules and Articles of War, which are statutory provisions modifying the laws of war only in the particular cases to which these provisions apply. In all cases not embraced in this statutory law and not made triable by the courts, which it creates, we must recur to the general code of war and try by a military commission.

A military commission will be immediately ordered to assemble at La Mine cantonment for the trial of such prisoners as may be brought before it. You will furnish the Judge

Advocate with a copy of this letter for his guidance and will see that the charges and specifications are properly drawn up.

Very respectfully, your obedient servant,
H. W. Halleck,
Major General.

In an effort to prevent any future mistakes, the leaders of the Union Army tried to send out orders that would put all military commands in the state on the same page of the military court manual when it came to the conduct of a trial. Unlike the civilian world where the experienced judge waited for the next defendant, the military world passed the experience around. Or better stated, any Union officer could find himself serving on the board of a military court. This created the need for thousands of officers in the Department of Missouri to have the exact same instructions for service on a commission.

GENERAL ORDERS No. 1.
HDQRS DEPARTMENT OF THE MISSOURI,
Saint Louis, January 1, 1862.

I. In carrying on war in a portion of country occupied or threatened to be attacked by an enemy, whether within or without the territory of the United States, crimes and military offenses are frequently committed which are not triable or punishable by courts-martial and which are not within the jurisdiction of any existing civil court. Such cases, however, must be investigated and the guilty parties punished. The good of society and the safety of the army imperiously demand this, they must therefore be taken cognizance of by the military power, but except in cases of extreme urgency a military commander should not himself attempt to decide upon the guilt or innocence of individuals. On the contrary it is the usage and custom of war among all civilized nations to refer such cases to a duly constituted military tribunal composed of reliable officers, who acting under the solemnity of an oath and the responsibility always attached to a court of record will examine witnesses, determine the guilt or innocence of parties accused and fix the punishment. This is usually done by courts-martial; but in our country these courts have a very limited jurisdiction both in regard to persons and offenses. Many classes of persons cannot be arraigned before such courts for any offense whatsoever, and many crimes committed even by military officers, enlisted men or camp retainers cannot be tried under the Rules and Articles of War Military commissions must be resorted to for such cases and these commissions should be ordered by the same authority, be constituted in a similar manner and their proceedings be conducted according to the same general rules as courts-martial in order to prevent abuses which might otherwise arise.

II. As much misapprehension has arisen in this department in relation to this subject the following rules are published for the information of all concerned:

First. Military commissions can be ordered only by the General-in-Chief of the Army or by the commanding officer of the department, and the proceedings must be sent to headquarters for revision.

Second. They will be composed of not less than three members, one of whom will act as Judge Advocate and recorder where no officer is designated for that duty. A larger number will be detailed where the public service will permit.

Third. All the proceedings will be recorded and signed by the President and Judge Advocate and recorder as in the case of courts-martial. These proceedings will be governed by the same rules as courts-martial so far as they may be applicable.

Fourth. A military commission will not try civil offenses cognizable by civil courts whenever such loyal courts exist. It should therefore be stated in every application for a commission whether or not there is any loyal civil court to which the civil offenses charge can be referred for trial. It must be observed, however, that many offenses, which in time of peace are civil offenses, become in time of war military offenses and are to be tried by a military tribunal even in places where civil tribunals exist.

Fifth. No case, which by the Rules and Articles of War is triable by a court-martial, will be tried by a military commission. Charges therefore preferred against prisoners before a military commission should be violation of the laws of war, and never violation of the Rules and Articles of War, which are statutory provisions defining and modifying the general laws of war in particular cases and in regard to particular persons and offenses. They do not apply to cases not embraced in the statute; but all cases so embraced must be tried by a court-martial. In other cases, we must be governed by the general code of war.

Sixth. Treason as a distinct offense is defined by the Constitution and must be tried by courts duly constituted by law; but certain acts of a treasonable character such as conveying information to the enemy, acting as spies, & etc., are military offenses triable by military tribunals and punishable by military authority.

Seventh. The fact that those persons who are now carrying on hostilities against the lawful authorities of the United States are rebels and traitors to the Government does not deprive them of any of the fights of war so far as the military authorities are concerned. In our intercourse with the duly authorized forces of the so-called Confederate States" and in the treatment of prisoners of war taken from such forces we must be governed by the usages and customs of war in like cases. But the rights so given to such prisoners by the laws of war do not according to the same code exempt them from trial and punishment by the proper courts for treason or other offenses against the Government. The rights which they may very properly claim as belligerents under the general rules of belligerent intercourse — commercial belli — cannot exempt them from the punishment to which they may have subjected themselves as citizens under the general laws of the land.

> *Eighth. Again, a soldier duly enrolled and authorized to act in a military capacity in the enemy's service is not according to the code military individually responsible for the taking of human life in battle, siege, & etc., while at the same time he is held individually responsible for any act which he may commit in violation of the laws of war. Thus, he cannot be punished by a military tribunal for committing acts of hostility, which are authorized by the laws of war, but if he has committed murder, robbery, theft, arson, & etc., the fact of his being a prisoner of war does not exempt him from trial by a military tribunal.*
>
> *Ninth. And again, while the code of war gives certain exemptions to a soldier regularly in the military service of an enemy it is a well-established principle that insurgents not militarily organized under the laws of the State, predatory partisans and guerrilla bands are not entitled to such exemptions; such men are not legitimately in arms and the military name and garb which they have assumed cannot give a military exemption to the crimes which they may commit. They are in a legal sense mere freebooters and banditti and are liable to the same punishment, which was imposed upon guerrilla bands by Napoleon in Spain, and by Scott in Mexico.*
>
> *By Order of Major General Halleck:*
> *JNO. C. KELTON,*
> *Assistant Adjutant General*

Now that all Union officers were hopefully on the same page of instructions, it was time to begin to work. In December of 1861, MG Halleck issued General Orders No. 32, which focused on the destruction of railroads and telegraph lines in the state. There had been a large number of arrests for these violations and a number of defendants waited for their trials. Many of these trials were very short in length and featured very fast work to determine justice. In this first case against William Combs, the trial action was quick with only two witnesses to testify.

DANVILLE, MONTGOMERY COUNTY, MO.,

January 31, 1862.

The military commission met pursuant to adjournment.

Present: Lt. Colonel Samuel A. Holmes, Tenth Missouri Volunteers; Captain Richard Y. Lanius, Eighty-first Ohio Volunteers; Captain A. G. Todd, Tenth Missouri Volunteers; Captain M. Armstrong, Judge Advocate, Eighty-first Ohio Volunteers.

William Combs, the accused, also present.

The Judge Advocate having read the order convening the court asked the accused, William Combs, if he had any objection to any member named thereon; to which he replied, "I have not."

The commission was then duly sworn by the Judge Advocate and the Judge Advocate was duly sworn by the presiding officer of the court in the presence of the accused.

The accused here, by permission of the commission, introduced Walter L. Lovelace, esq., as his counsel.

The charges were then read aloud by the Judge Advocate as follows:

CHARGE 1: Destroying railroads and railroad property.

Specification: In this, that the said William Combs on or about the twentieth day of December, A.D. 1861, at the town of Wellsville in the county of Montgomery in the State of Missouri and within the lines occupied by the troops of the United States did unlawfully, willfully and maliciously tear up, burn and destroy the rails, railroad ties, track, bridges, depots and other buildings of the North Missouri Railroad (so-called) and the property of said railroad company contrary to the laws and customs of war in like cases.

CHARGE 2: Destroying telegraph lines.

Specification: In this, that the said William Combs on or about the twentieth day of December, 1861, at the town of Wellsville in the county of Montgomery in the State of Missouri and within the line occupied by the troops of the United

States did unlawfully, willfully and maliciously cut down and destroy the telegraph wires and poles and burn and destroy the telegraph office at the town of Wellsville of the U.S. military telegraph along the line of the North Missouri Railroad in said town of Wellsville and county of Montgomery contrary to the laws and customs of war in like cases.

M. ARMSTRONG,
Captain and Judge Advocate.

The Judge Advocate then asked the accused, William Combs, you have heard the charges preferred against you; how say you, guilty or not guilty?

To which the accused, William Combs, pleaded as follows: To specification to first charge, not guilty. To charge one, not guilty. To specification to second charge, not guilty. To charge two, not guilty.

The commission then proceeded in the examination of the case of William Combs, as follows:

BENTLY HAYS, a citizen of the county of Callaway in the State of Missouri, being produced, duly sworn and examined on the part of the United States testifies as follows:

I know the prisoner, William Combs. I have known him some eight or ten years. He lives in Montgomery County, Missouri. I think he lives close to Montgomery City. He belonged to Meyers' company. He was with us at the time we were at the brick-kiln at Mr. Wingfield's. He met with us in the old house at Laile's pasture, and then came down with us to Mr. Wingfield's. We met at Laile's pasture the day before the night on which the railroad was torn up. I think there was between fifty and a hundred who met at Laile's pasture before going to Wingfield's. From Laile's pasture we went down to Wingfield's brick-kiln at which place we stayed something like half an hour or three-quarters. From there, we all went to the section-house between the towns of Montgomery and Wellsville. The defendant was along. At the section-house we went to tearing up the railroad. We did not destroy the section.

We tore up about one hundred yards of the railroad track at this place. I think defendant assisted to tear up the track; some held horses. We had mauls, such as we make rails with, and some crowbars. We got some crowbars at the section-house. From the section-house we went toward Wellsville. We would tear up a place, then miss a distance, and then tear up again. We went to Wellsville, and met a company coming down. We cut down the telegraph poles, cut the wires off the poles, and burnt the poles. When we met the other party, we all went to Wellsville, or most of us. When we went into Wellsville some went to loading up wagons from the store of Kapinska, of that place; others went to the depot of that place and burnt it and cut down the flagpoles. I saw the defendant there. There was some shouting and cheering. I think we stayed at Wellsville an hour — maybe more. Some of us went with Meyers back to Montgomery City, and I judge others went home. The defendant went back to Montgomery with me. James Morris, Mr. Smith, and Mr. Hawkins went back to Montgomery City with us. There were several of us — I can't remember. The last I saw of Mr. Combs he was going toward the grocery at Montgomery City. I think the next time I saw defendant was at my own house. I do not know whether defendant went home after the railroad was destroyed. Defendant went, and I saw him afterward with Meyers' company at Laile's pasture.

Cross-examined by DEFENDANT'S ATTORNEY:

Q: Was defendant a member of Meyers' company?

A: Yes, Sir, he was.

Q: When and where was he sworn in?

A: I could not be certain, but I think he was sworn in on the thirteenth of December last at George Harvey's.

Q: Was Meyers a commissioned officer in the Confederate service?

A: I do not know whether he was or not. I should judge though that he was; I don't know for certain.

Q: Were Meyers' men sworn into the Confederate service or what is called the Missouri State Guard?

A: I could not be positive about that. I think it was the Missouri State Guard.

Q: Was Meyers acting commanding officer of that company?

A: He was.

Q: Was the railroad and telegraph destroyed by his orders?

A: What we destroyed was done under Meyers' orders.

Q: Was the defendant engaged in destroying the railroad and telegraph on that night?

A: Yes, I think he was. He was along. Some of the men held horses. I think, though, he helped destroy the railroad.

Q: About how many of the men were engaged in holding horses?

A: I could not say exactly. I judge there were about five men more or less.

Q: Reflect and see if the defendant was not one of those five?

A: I could not say for certain whether he was or not.

Q: Were those holding horses in the immediate vicinity of those tearing up the road?

A: They were tolerably close by.

Q: When did Meyers first tell his men that they intended to destroy the railroad?

A: At the kiln near Mr. Wingfield's on the evening of the night it was done.

Q: Was the defendant present at that time?

A: Yes, I think he was. I could not say for certain, but I think he was.

Q: Was the matter of tearing up the railroad spoken of at any time on your way from the brick-kiln to the railroad?

A: Not that I recollect of.

Q: Was it spoken of at any time before you got to the brick-kiln?

A: If it was I never heard it. I knew nothing of it 'til we got to the brick-kiln.

Q: In what way was it made known at the brick-kiln that their intention was to tear up the railroad on that night?

A: Mr. Meyers told us at that time and I think he said it was his orders.

Q: Was it told to the whole company present at that time?

A: I think all were present. He told it out so all could understand.

By the COURT:

Q: After the time you met at Harvey's house, did the company keep together or did they go home?

A: They went home.

Q: These men dispersed always when they met and met when called together, I suppose?

A: Yes, Sir.

Q: How many times did they meet from the time they were sworn in until the time the railroad was destroyed?

A: I think they met but once — at Laile's pasture.

JOHN R. HAYDEN being produced, sworn and examined on the part of the United States says:

I know the defendant, William Combs. I have known him about two months. The first time I saw him was at a party on Loutre Creek in the edge of Callaway. It was at a kind of a dance. He lives in Montgomery County; I don't know exactly where, I was never at his house. I live in Montgomery City. He belonged to Meyers' company, or was with it. I did not see him sworn in; I couldn't say for that. I first saw him with Meyers' company at headquarters in Laile's pasture. I think he was there the evening we met when we tore up the road. We went from Laile's pasture to the brick-kiln at Wingfield's place. These meetings were to organize. I was there at Laile's but twice — the time that we met to destroy the road, and the time we met to leave the country. I suppose there were about thirty at the brick-kiln; I did not count. I think the defendant was there. We went to the section-house on the railroad above Montgomery City and commenced tearing up the road. We tore up the road in three or four different places between that and Wellsville and also at the section-house. The defendant was along with us while we were at that work; I could not say I saw him at work but I know he was along. At Wellsville, we burnt up the depot, and then came back to Montgomery City, and from there went home I suppose. I did not go with them to Montgomery City; I went back into Callaway County. I was kicking around; I did not stay at any particular place. Defendant was with us when we were last at Laile's pasture and went off with the company, and so did I.

Cross-examined by DEFENDANT'S COUNSEL:

Q: Where did you meet the defendant on the night of the destruction of the railroad?

A: At the brick-kiln in the bottom.

Q: To what point on the railroad did you go from the brick-kiln?

A: To that section-house between Montgomery City and Wellsville.

Q: Which way did you go?

A: Out the road toward Wellsville.

Q: Where did you first commence?

A: At the section-house.

Q: Were all or part engaged on the railroad to hold horses?

A: Yes, there was a part.

Q: Was the defendant holding horses, or at work on the railroad?

A: I don't know; I could not say. I did not see whether he was holding horses or at work.

Q: Did you see the defendant on the railroad at all?

A: Yes, Sir, he was.

Q: Where was he?

A: I saw him in Wellsville and I saw him as he came back.

Q: What was he doing?

A: He was on his horse riding round and came back with the crowd. I could not say I saw him at work but I know that he was along.

Q: Did you see him at any time while you were tearing up the railroad?

A: I can't say; I might and might not. I can't say that I saw him at work.

Q: Where did you meet with Meyers' company?

A: At Laile's pasture.

Q: Which way was the defendant going when you saw him at the brick-kiln?

A: He went with us out toward the road on the prairie.

Q: Did he come to you before or after Meyers told you were going to destroy the railroad?

A: Before.

Q: Where did you next see him?

A: On the prairie going along toward the railroad.

Q: Did you see him at any time when you were destroying the railroad?

A: I might and I might not. I did not take notice.

Re-examined:

I think he was along with us while we were destroying the road.

The counsel for defense declined to file any statement on the part of defense but referred the court to the statement in the case of the United States against Norris.

The testimony in this case is here closed and case submitted. The proceedings were read over and the statement of the parties being in possession of the court the court was cleared for deliberation and having maturely considered the evidence adduced find the accused, William Combs, as follows:

Of charge one, guilty. Of specification, charge one, guilty. Of charge two, guilty. Of specification, charge two, guilty.

And the commission does therefore sentence the said William Combs to be shot to death at such time and place, as the commanding general shall direct.

The above is a full and complete record of the proceedings, finding and sentence of the military commission in the case of William Combs.

SAMUEL A. HOLMES,

Lieutenant Colonel, and President of Commission.

M. ARMSTRONG,

Captain, Judge Advocate and Recorder Military Commission.

Finding approved and the sentence will be carried into effect at a time and place to be hereafter designated by the general commanding the department. In the meantime, prisoner will be kept in close confinement in military prison at Alton.

H. W. HALLECK,

Major General.

Though the trials moved swiftly outcomes were not always predictable, as the next case demonstrates. This railroad destruction order case features a somewhat different ending. The Union officers involved here appear to have been men of mercy, or maybe they found the circumstances to be a little different.

SPECIAL ORDERS No. 81.

HEADQUARTERS DEPARTMENT OF THE MISSOURI,

Saint Louis, December 21, 1861.

A military commission is hereby appointed to meet in this city on Monday, the 23d instant, at 10 a.m., or as soon thereafter as practicable, for the trial of such persons as may be brought before it.

Detail for the commission: Brig. Gen. S. D. Sturgis, U.S. Army; Col. R. D. Cutts, of the staff; Lt. Col. John Scott. Third Iowa Volunteers; Maj. E. W. Chamberlain, First Iowa Cavalry; Capt. T. W. Sweeny, Second Infantry, U.S. Army. Col. R. D. Cutts will act as Judge Advocate and recorder.

By order of Major General Halleck:
J. C. KELTON,
Assistant Adjutant General.

SAINT LOUIS, Mo., January 10, 1862 — 10 a.m.

The commission met pursuant to adjournment and the above order. Present: Brig. Gen. S. D. Sturgis, U.S. Army; Col. R. D. Cutts, of the staff; Lt. Col. John Scott, Third Iowa Volunteers; Maj. E. W. Chamberlain, First Iowa Cavalry.

The accused, William Hearst, and his counsel also present.

The Judge Advocate having read the order convening the commission asked the accused, William Hearst if he had any objection to any member named therein, to which he replied that he had not. The commission was then sworn by the Judge Advocate, the Judge Advocate taking the oath at the same time as a member of the commission in the presence of the accused.

The accused was then arraigned upon the following charge and specification, which were read aloud to the commission by the Judge Advocate:

CHARGE: Violation of the laws of war.

Specification: In this, that he, William Hearst, of Jefferson County, Missouri did aid and assist in the burning of the Iron Mountain Railroad Bridge across Big River, Jefferson County, Missouri, thus risking and putting in jeopardy the lives of innocent persons traveling on said road, the same being done in violation of the laws and usages of war. This on or about the sixteenth of October, 1861.

The Judge Advocate then addressed the accused as follows: You, William Hearst, have heard the charge and specification preferred against you; how say you, guilty or not guilty?

To which arraignment the accused pleaded as follows:

To the specification, not guilty.

To the charge, not guilty.

JOHN W. WILSON, a witness for the prosecution, was duly sworn.

By the Judge Advocate:

Q: State your name, residence, and occupation.

A: John W. Wilson; reside at Big River Bridge, Jefferson County, Missouri; am a farmer.

Q: Do you know the accused, and if so how long have you known him?

A: I know him, and have been acquainted with him for about fourteen years, but during four and one-half years of that time I was in California. I was in California from 1852 to 1856.

Q: Since your return have you been in the habit of seeing him often, and how far did he live from your house?

A: He lived about eight or nine miles from my house, and I have often seen him at Morse's store and at post-office formerly kept at our house, and also at place where the post-office now is.

Q: Were you at home at the burning of Big River Bridge, and how far did you live from it?

A: I was. I lived about one-hundred fifty yards from it.

Q: Did you witness the burning of the bridge?

A: I saw it — the bridge on fire and the setting fire to the bridge. Before the burning of the bridge, I was arrested by a man who called himself Jeff Thompson. He released me, however, when some men spoke to him and told him I was a farmer who lived there. At the moment of my release I was about two-hundred yards from the bridge. I then met men coming with fire toward the bridge and I said to them, "For God's sake, don't burn the bridge; it will break us citizens up." I recognized no one among the men going with firebrands in their hand toward the bridge, but Mr. William Hearst. The firebrand held by him was about one and one-half feet long. I then turned 'round and seeing some men taking my rails I went after them to prevent them, when they cursed me. As I went down to our house I met Perkins, and I looked back and saw the bridge on fire and a lot of men around the bridge — say twenty or twenty-five men — some standing on the bridge, the flames a-blazing up on the sides, and other men standing on the embankment on Jefferson County side. There were also about twenty-five men on the other side of bridge beating and hammering, as if they were tearing up the track. I then went to our house and stayed there about one and one-half to two hours and then went from our house to Blackwell Station, Saint Francois County. There I met a lot of men, citizens of the county, who had come in on hearing the firing. Saw bodies of two secessionists lying on the platform who had been killed by Lippincott's men. Captain Lippincott [Illinois volunteers] had come to re-enforce Captain Elliott's company at the bridge. There had been a fight early in the morning, about seven a.m., between Captain Elliott's company and the secessionists, and the former, about forty in number, were taken prisoners by the latter. The secessionists then moved toward Blackwell Station where they were met by Captain Lippincott, both parties firing. I did not see but heard the firing. The bridge was burnt about eight a.m. about the fifteenth of October 1861. The bridge was burned while some of the secessionists, mostly cavalry, were on their way to Blackwell Station.

By the ACCUSED:

Q: Were there any officers in command of the men who burned the bridge?

A: I suppose there were. Some had swords, some had long knives. Heard an order given by one man with Captain's straps on his shoulder and saw the order obeyed.

Q: Do you belong to any secret order or society of men by which you are bound by oath to do all in your power to punish Hearst as a deserter from the army of Jeff Thompson?

A: I decline to answer.

By the COMMISSION:

Q: How near to bridge was accused when you saw him with firebrand in his hand, and did you see him apply the torch?

A: He was about thirty or forty yards from bridge. I spoke to him as he passed. Other men had just preceded him fifteen or twenty steps with firebrands in their hands. I did not know who they were. I did not see him apply the torch.

Q: Were the secessionists in uniform, or part of them only, and what proportion so far as you could judge?

A: I did not see any persons in uniform except the person who called himself Jeff Thompson and the Captain I have alluded to. The best part of them had overcoats on of different colors, and may have had uniforms on under them, for all I know.

There being no further questions to propose to the witness the evidence he had given was read to him and he was dismissed.

WILLIAM BLACKWELL, a witness for the prosecution, was duly sworn.

By the Judge Advocate:

Q: State your name, occupation, and residence.

A: William Blackwell, of Saint Francois County; a farmer, and reside on Iron Mountain Railroad.

Q: How far do you live from Big River Bridge?

A: Some three or four hundred yards southeast of bridge.

Q: Do you know the accused, and how long have you known him, and were you accustomed to see him often?

A: Yes; some ten or twelve years. Saw him occasionally, at one time frequently, and at another time, when he moved to a greater distance, not so often.

Q: Were you present at the burning of the Big River Bridge?

A: I was not at the bridge, but saw it from my house a-burning.

Q: Did you see any person engaged in the burning of bridge?

A: Yes, Sir. I saw a good many men running down from the camp which they had captured on the hill, with something in their hands emitting smoke; appeared to be on fire. I was so far off I could not see the fire itself. I did not recognize Mr. Hearst in that crowd; I was so far off — three or four hundred yards — I could not recognize him, but recognized him after the bridge was on fire, in the crowd going down the railroad line, and that was the last time I saw Mr. Hearst until he was a prisoner.

Q: How far were you from the accused when you recognized him?

A: I was close to him — a few paces off — as he passed my house. Can't say whether he was armed or not. He was going southward when I saw him. There had been a light in the morning before bridge was burned between Jeff Thompson's men and Captain Elliott. The latter were taken prisoners and disarmed after the fight at the bridge and the burning of it. There was also a fight at Blackwell Station.

Q: Did the fight at Blackwell take place after the bridge was burned?

A: After, Sir; the firing was heard by me after I saw the bridge on fire.

By the ACCUSED:

Q: About how many men composed the army or company, which passed your house going from the bridge?

A: I suppose there were about one-hundred forty or one-hundred fifty men.

Q: Was any portion of railroad track torn up on the south, Saint Francois side of the bridge?

A: I think there were a few rails torn up.

There being no further questions to propose to the witness, the evidence he had given was read to him and he was dismissed.

The examination by the prosecution was here closed.

HENRY P. BATES, a witness for the defense, was duly sworn.

By the ACCUSED:

Q: Are you acquainted with me?

A: Yes, I have known him since a boy.

Q: At what time did you see me last before my arrest, and where?

A: I saw him about the fifth of November at my place of doing business, called Morse's Mills, on Big River, Jefferson County, Missouri.

Q: Did you request Captain Dover or other U.S. Officer to arrest me, and at whose request did you do so, and for what reason?

A: I wrote to Captain Dover to go and arrest Mr. Hearst at his own solicitation. The reason, as he told me, using his own expression — that he had joined Jeff Thompson's army; that he was not going back there, and wished to be arrested as a prisoner of war of the United States; also, that he wished to avail himself of the ordinance of the State convention and of the proclamation of Governor Gamble. The reason of his request to be arrested instead of giving himself up, as he stated, was that he feared the punishment that would be inflicted on him as a deserter in case he should fall into the hands of the rebel army.

Q: Did Captain Dover arrest me? If not, why?

A: No, Sir; Captain Dover, being absent from his post, did not get my letter before he was arrested by Captain Miller, of the detective police.

Q: Did I go voluntarily to you and propose my arrest, and where was I arrested?

A: He came voluntarily to me and asked me if I could not have him arrested. I cannot say of my own knowledge where he was arrested; but before leaving I said to him, "William, where will you be found in case I send someone to arrest you?" And he answered that he would be found at home. At the time alluded to, Mr. Hearst appeared quite penitent and could not speak of the subject without tears. I was not aware, at the time, that he was in the neighborhood.

Q: Do you know my past reputation as a citizen? And if so, what has it been?

A: I have known Mr. Hearst for a long time; his general reputation was good — a good neighbor and fast friend when he was attached to any person. In point of education, very limited. He seldom reads. I would state that the present position of Mr. Hearst before this court was brought about by my advice to him.

By the Judge Advocate:

Q: Was he at home or in such position in regard to U.S. forces that he could or would have been arrested whether you had written to Captain Dover or not?

A: If he had not followed my advice and gone home he could have avoided being arrested.

Q: Was he within the lines of the U.S. forces at that time?

A: Yes, Sir.

There being no further questions to propose to witness the evidence he had given was read to him and he was dismissed.

JOHN TOMBS, a witness for defense, was duly sworn.

By the ACCUSED:

Q: Are you acquainted with me?

A: Not personally.

Q: State your knowledge of my acts showing an intention to avail myself of the benefit of the amnesty provided by the ordinance of the Missouri State convention passed on sixteenth of October 1861, before the time of my arrest.

A: On or about the third of November last, the brother of the accused came to me and said that he and his brother had come home with the intention of staying at home. He requested me to go to see Colonel Lawson the next morning (Monday) and state to Lawson that they had come home with the intention of staying, and to ask his advice whether they had better deliver themselves up to him or to troops at Big River bridge. I went to Lawson next morning, and he said he would go with Shem up to the forge at Pilot Knob, if they would go up there with him. He said that if they would deliver themselves up as prisoners of war he would take them up to Pilot Knob. He told me to go back and tell them to keep out of the road until he could go up with them, as he had to go to Saint Louis, and would not be able to go up with them for a few days. I came back about one or two o'clock same day and told George Hearst, brother of accused, the message Colonel Lawson sent, and to tell his brother to keep out of the way until he, Lawson, returned from Saint Louis, for the reason that the troops at Big River Bridge would treat him very roughly if they took him. There was a sick child at George's house, so that he could not go down to his brother William's house until Wednesday morning, and in the meantime, they came and took his brother. The brother of accused came back the same evening and told me that his brother William was taken. George Hearst delivered himself up to Colonel Lawson, took the oath of allegiance, and is now at home with a pass. Colonel Lawson belongs to U.S. forces.

There being no further questions to propose to the witness the evidence he had given was read to him and he was dismissed.

WILLIAM BLACKWELL, a witness for the prosecution, recalled.

By the Judge Advocate:

Q: Was Big River Bridge the day before or some time previous to its being burned within the lines of the U.S. forces?

A: Yes, there were U.S. troops to the southward of bridge.

Evidence read to witness by Judge Advocate and he was dismissed.

The accused represented to the commission that an important witness in his behalf was not in the city of Saint Louis, but would be here in two days; and having satisfied the commission that the evidence expected from said witness was necessary for his proper defense the case was postponed to Monday, January 13, at 10 a.m.

The commission then adjourned to meet tomorrow, Saturday, January 11, at 10 a.m.

SAINT LOUIS, MO., January 11, 1862 — 10 a.m.

The commission met pursuant to adjournment, all the members present.

The absence of Captain T. W. Sweeny, Second Infantry, U.S. Army, on yesterday was due to the fact as stated by him that he presented himself to the sentinels on Gratiot Street, the route usually taken by members of the commission to their office, for the purpose of proceeding to the said office and to the performance of his duties when he was stopped by the sentinels; and when he informed them that he was a member of the military commission they still refused to let him pass and he therefore turned back.

There being no business before the commission it adjourned to meet on Monday, January 13, 1862, at 10 a.m.

SAINT LOUIS, MO., January 13, 1862 — 10 a.m.

The commission met pursuant to adjournment, all the members present.

The accused, William Hearst, also present.

The proceedings of January 10 and 11 were read over to the commission by the Judge Advocate.

THOMAS E. MOTHERSHEAD, a witness for the defense, was duly sworn.

By the ACCUSED:

Q: State your name, residence, and occupation.

A: Thomas E. Mothershead, lives within eight miles of Hillsborough, western part of Jefferson County, Missouri; a farmer.

Q: Do you know me, and how long have you known me?

A: We were boys raised together, and I am thirty-two years old. We lived within one and a half miles of each other until we were married.

Q: Have you any knowledge of my enlistment as a soldier in the army of Jeff Thompson, and if so, when and where did the enlistment occur?

A: I have some knowledge of it. I was in Bloomfield, Stoddard County, Missouri, and went down to the camp of Colonel Lowe's regiment, in Jeff Thompson's army and there I saw William Hearst and several others whom I knew, and Hearst told me that he was going to enlist and asked me to go up with him. We went up together to the headquarters of Colonel Lowe, and there Colonel Lowe swore him in as a private soldier in my presence. I saw him after that several times in the company to which he belonged.

Q: State the reputation as a citizen I have hitherto enjoyed, and also any knowledge you may have of the influences brought to bear upon me to induce me to go into the rebellion.

A: He was a citizen of Jefferson County, a farmer, peaceable as any man you could pick out down there; reputation as good and honest as any man in the country. I have seen William Hearst there frequently in county; and there were some men in the home guards at De Soto who did not like Hearst, and would report that he (Hearst) had been drilling there for the purpose of whipping the home guard, and through their influence and action he became satisfied that his life was in danger if he stayed there. He thought so and so expressed himself to me. He told me that was the cause of his going down to the army, and he said after he got down there that if he thought the men of the home guard would not pester or molest him he would go back home and stay there, and would have nothing to do with Jeff Thompson's army. We had frequent conversations on the subject before he left, and he always expressed these sentiments. He was a man that would rather do anything else than leave home; always talked in that way — that is, that he would not leave home unless afeared of persecution by some men of the home guard. One of these men was a cousin of Hearst's, and had been hired by him as a farm hand, and he would not work unless William Hearst was with him, and William discharged him, and he consequently became an enemy.

Q: Were you in Jefferson County at the time the bridge over Big River was burned?

A: No, Sir; I was not.

Q: Have you any knowledge of the fight at Big River Bridge or at Blackwell Station on or about October sixteenth, 1861, and whether the burning of said bridge by Jeff Thompson and his men was necessary to affect their escape or not?

A: I have no knowledge of the fight, or of the burning of the bridge except from hearsay.

By the Judge Advocate:

Q: Do you know the names of the officers in command or the name of the regiment in which the accused enlisted at Bloomfield?

A: I know some of them. The captain's name was White, and the first lieutenant's name was Whittaker Martin. It was a cavalry company attached to Colonel Lowe's regiment, under Jeff Thompson.

Q: What was the date of the enlistment of the accused?

A: I think it was between the middle and the last of September, 1861.

Q: You say that the accused, William Hearst, had been reported by some men of the home guard at De Soto as drilling men to whip the home guard; do you know whether this accusation was true or false?

A: It was false to my personal knowledge. I know he never did; he could not do it.

There being no further questions to propose to the witness the evidence he had given was read to him by the Judge Advocate and the witness dismissed.

The examination by the defense was here closed. The accused then presented his written defense, appended to these proceedings and marked A, which was read to the commission by the Judge Advocate.

The commission was then cleared for deliberation, and having maturely weighed and considered the evidence adduced find the accused, William Hearst, of Jefferson County, Missouri, as follows:

Of the specification, guilty.

Of the charge, guilty.

And the commission does therefore sentence the said William Hearst, of Jefferson County, Missouri, to be shot to death.

S. D. STURGIS,

Brigadier General, U.S. Army.

RICH'D D. CUTTS,

Colonel, U.S. Army, and Judge Advocate.

The commission then adjourned to meet tomorrow, Tuesday, January 14, 1862, at 10 a.m.

The commission having thus performed the painful duty of awarding punishment in conformity to the laws of war and to General Orders No. 32, 1861, which deprived them of all discretionary power, beg leave to recommend the case of William Hearst to the merciful consideration of the confirming authority.

The members of the commission engaged in the trial have reason to believe that the prisoner is an unusually stupid and ignorant man, and not capable of discriminating between the lawful commands of a superior officer and those that are criminal; that he enlisted in the rebel ranks more from unfounded fear of his neighbors than from any deep-seated feeling of disloyalty, and that he voluntarily delivered himself up as a prisoner when he could have escaped arrest.

S. D. STURGIS,

Brigadier General, U.S. Army.

RICH'D D. CUTTS,

Colonel, U.S. Army, and Judge Advocate.

JOHN SCOTT,

Lieutenant Colonel, Third Iowa Infantry.
E. W. CHAMBERLAIN,
Major, First Iowa Cavalry.

EXHIBIT A.

Being illiterate I was made the dupe of bad men who have hitherto borne such a good name in my neighborhood that I was led to place confidence in them. I never entertained a thought of overthrowing the Government, but went to Thompson's army through fear of Federal troops whom I was induced to believe were coming upon me and my neighbors with fire and the sword to commit an indiscriminate slaughter. I was told and believed that the Federal troops were usurping authority and destroying the guarantees of the Constitution. Thus misled, I went to Jeff Thompson's rebel army, who I believed were fighting for the Constitution against usurpation of the President.

The evidence shows that I there enlisted in a company organized as I understood by authority of the laws of the State of Missouri. Being regularly mustered into the said army I became subject to the orders of the officers of the company and battalion. We were ordered to march up to the Big River Bridge. We were told that the destruction of that bridge was a military necessity, and were ordered by our officers under the penalties inflicted by military law for disobedience of orders to destroy the bridge. I felt it was wrong at the time, and hesitated. The bridge was fired by others not by myself. The statements of the witness Wilson are untrue. He was present at the burning of the bridge and was as active as any of the men of Thompson, and as much rejoiced at our success. A confrère and associate of the leading secessionists in Jefferson County before that time, his hesitancy and refusal to answer as to his membership of the order of Knights of the Golden Circle must be satisfactory to the court of his complicity with the schemes of the rebellion and the wicked purposes of his statements. The evidence shows how I returned to my home as soon as I found that I could do so and as soon as it was shown to my understanding how greatly I had been duped.

The proof shows that I returned and offered to comply with the provisions of the ordinance of the Missouri State convention to obtain the amnesty there offered. This I was prevented from doing by my arrest and imprisonment. I did hesitate to go voluntarily and surrender myself; I knew the fearful punishment which the members of the order of the Knights of the Golden Circle were sworn to visit upon a deserter from the rebel army and I therefore requested Mr. Bates and sent for Colonel Lawson to send and have me arrested.

In good faith I laid down my arms, relying upon the amnesty promised by the convention and which I am informed the President of the United States has recognized and agreed to respect. I have been humbugged into the folly and crime of rebellion. I saw the deception practiced upon me, and felt the folly and crime I had been guilty of. I sought to return to my allegiance. I was assured of safety in so doing. I would not have been taken had I not desired it. The proof shows this. My hands bear no stains of blood. I was never in a battle. All that I did was in a regular manner of regular warfare. If I am not permitted to return to my allegiance under the provisions of the ordinance of the convention I am still entitled to the treatment of a prisoner of war. This I do not desire as I do not wish to be exchanged. I submit my fate to this commission. If the punishment I have endured be not sufficient for unintentional crime I have been guilty of toward my country I am willing to endure more. What I may not ask of the justice of the commission I may entreat of its mercy that I may be permitted to return to my allegiance lay home and my family, and by future loyalty and devotion to the Constitution and Union of the United States endeavor to atone for the error of the past.

WILLIAM HEARST.

The finding and sentence are approved; but in consideration of the recommendation of the members of the commission, on account of the general ignorance and stupidity of the prisoner the sentence is mitigated to confinement in the military prison during the war.

H. W. HALLECK,
Major General.

Chapter 3.

The Misguided Husband

United States v. Francis M. Musgrave

A citizen of Pulaski County Missouri

The American Civil War introduced a period of widespread suffering and heartbreak to many American families. The much-used quote of "a house divided" can't capture the strain some men placed upon their families. The most common cause of grief was death or a crippling injury to the soldier. But there were many other ways to create intense pain and suffering. This chapter tells the story of a family in deep trouble. It features a young wife left at home with her small child, while her husband goes off to war. Then add a misguided and confused husband who did not seem to understand the war. Account for the extended family members who were already in the war, and you'll find this story to be an interesting mess. This chapter documents the extraordinary steps one young wife had to take to save her husband.

On April 1, 1863, the Headquarters of the Union Department of Missouri by Special Order No. 86, directed six army officers to convene as a military commission in St. Louis, Missouri on Tuesday April 7,1863, or "as soon thereafter as practicable, for the trial of such persons as may be brought before it." One of the cases to come before the board was titled "Francis M. Musgrave, a citizen of Pulaski County Missouri."

The trial of Musgrave began on May 18,1863 at 10:30 a.m. at an unknown military location in St. Louis Missouri. BG W. K. Strong was assigned as President of the Commission. The defendant, Francis M. Musgrave, was brought before the commission and heard the order read appointing the commission. The officers on the board were presented to Musgrave by name and rank. Musgrave was asked if he had any objection to any member named in the detail. The accused stated he had no objection to any member.

The officer who would record the trial, MAJ Allen Blacker, then swore in the members of the commission. The President of the Commission duly swore in the recorder. As required, all of this was done in the presence of the defendant. Musgrave was then arraigned by the commission on the charge and specification, Violation of the oath of allegiance to the United States Government.

For the benefit of the reader the exact order, which deals with the oath of allegiance that was used by the Union troops, was as follows:

> *GENERAL ORDERS No. 5.*
> *HEADQUARTERS SAINT LOUIS DISTRICT,*
> *Saint Louis, Mo., December 6, 1861.*
>
> *I. To carry out the arrangements for protecting the commerce of the Mississippi as required by General Orders No. 4. Of this district, the oath embodied in paragraph II and the blanks for names and description are prescribed for the use of the boats and houses engaged in this trade. This oath is also prescribed as the oath of allegiance to be taken and subscribed in obedience to paragraph V of General Orders No. 13, of the Department of the Missouri, and in all other cases in this command when an oath of allegiance is authorized and required.*
>
> *II. Oath of allegiance to the United States Government:*
>
> *I solemnly swear that I will hear true allegiance to the United States and support and sustain the Constitution and laws thereof; that I will maintain the national sovereignty paramount to that of all State, county or confederate powers; that I will discourage, discountenance and forever oppose secession, rebellion and disintegration of the Federal Union; that I disclaim and denounce all faith and fellowship with the so-called Confederate States and Confederate armies and pledge my honor, my property and my life to the sacred*

performance of this my solemn oath of allegiance to the Government of the United States of America.

By order of Brigadier General Curtis:

N. P. CHIPMAN,

Major and Acting Assistant Adjutant General.

The specification against Musgrave was very precise and detailed. The specification stated:

In this, that he the said Francis M. Musgrave did on or about the month of March 1862, take and subscribe the oath of allegiance to the United States Government before an officer duly authorized and empowered to administer the same; by the terms of which said oath F. M. Musgrave bound and obligated himself to support, protect, and defend the constitution and government of the United States and to bear true faith and allegiance and loyalty to the same — and afterwards did violate said oath of allegiance by joining with and enlisting in a company of rebels and being sworn in the service of the so-called confederate states for the term of three years in the company of Bradford in Pickett's Regiment, and did act therein as an enemy of the United States during the period of some four months, this in or about the month July 1862 in the county of Howell in the state of Missouri in violation of his oath of allegiance to the United States.

Having heard the charge and specification read in open court the defendant Francis M. Musgrave was asked to give his formal plea to the charge. Musgrave entered a plea of guilty to the charge. With a guilty plea, Musgrave ended the trial procedure. However, he did ask to read into the court record a statement in his own defense. The court agreed and Musgrave read the following statement to the court:

Statement of F. M. Musgrave, a prisoner at the Gratiot Street Military Prison, St. Louis, Missouri, made on the eleventh day of April 1863. My age is twenty-one years; I live in Pulaski County Missouri. I was born in Pulaski County.

I was surrendered in Howell County on or about the twelfth day of February 1863. A soldier in the Confederate

Army was the cause of my surrender. I was in arms against the United States and was a private in Captain Bradford's Company, Colonel Pickett's Regiment, and was sworn into the rebel service about the thirtieth day of July 1862 in Howell County, Missouri for three years. When surrendered, I was first taken to Ironton and remained there one week and was not examined there, [Author's note: he means questioned there] and was sent to Gratiot Street Prison around the twenty-seventh day of July 1863, and never took the oath of allegiance about [illegible] day of March 1862.

Musgrave continued the statement by saying:

I have been in arms once during the rebellion. I have served under Colonel Pickett. I have been in no battles or skirmishes. I had arms, was out on picket. [Author's note: picket is a guard or sentry post] I have never furnished arms, nor ammunition horse, or provisions, nor any kind of supplies to any rebels. There was no rebel camp near me that I did not give notice of to the United States troops. I have never been with anyone taking or keeping horse, ammo, or other property.

I am not enrolled in the E. M. M. [Author's note: Enrolled Missouri Militia, each side had their own enrolled army], loyal or disloyal. I did not want to fight [illegible] the rebels at that time. I am a southern sympathizer. I do not sincerely desire to have the southern people put down in this war, and the authority of the U.S. Government over these actions. I want them to have their rights. I have no slaves. I have a wife and one child. My occupation is farming. I have in the rebellion a brother, brothers-in-law, and cousins. I have been in no rebel camp but my own, was in from July 'til twentieth of December 1862, six months at different places. I stood guard. I was left sick at Vanburen one month. I started for home and while on my way I came to the Federal Army and was surrendered. I was aware that I was violating my oath when I joined the rebels. I preferred to fight with them. I do not want to be exchanged. [Author's note: he refers here to the exchange of prisoners between north and south] I would like to take the oath again. I do not want to enroll, because I do not want to fight against my relatives.

There was no rebel camp near me that I did
not give notice of to the United States troops.
I have never been with any one taking or
pressing horses, arms or other property.
I am not enrolled in the E.M.M. loyal or
disloyal. I did not want to fight with the
Federals at that time; I am a Southern
Sympathizer. I do not sincerely desire
to have the Southern people put down in this war,
and the authority of the U.S. Government over
them restored. I want them to have their
rights. I have no slaves. I have a wife
and one child. My occupation is farming.
I have in the Rebellion a brother, brother-in-law
Cousins. I have been in no rebel camp
but my own was in from July till 20th December 1862. Six months. at different places, stood
guard &c. I was left sick at Van Buren, I started
for home, and while on my way I came to the Federal
Army and surrendered. I was sick at Van Buren
one month. I was aware that I was violating my
oath, when I joined the rebels. I preferred to fight
them. I do not want to be Exchanged. I

THIS SAMPLE PAGE OF A HANDWRITTEN TRIAL RECORD IS FROM THE CASE OF FRANCIS M. MUSGRAVE, WHO VIOLATED HIS OATH OF ALLEGIANCE TO THE UNITED STATES GOVERNMENT BY JOINING THE REBEL ARMY.

Musgrave then told the court he had no witnesses to examine and he had no additional statements to make before the court. According to the trial record:

The court was then cleared for deliberation and having maturely considered the evidence adduced find the accused, Francis M. Musgrave as follows:

Of the specification of the charge, guilty. Of the charge, guilty. The commission do therefore sentence him, Francis M. Musgrave that he be shot to death at such time and place as the Major General Commanding the Department may direct. All the members of the commission concurring therein.

Following the verdict, Musgrave was sent back to the prison to wait while his case was appealed to a higher military authority. The next entry in the case record appears on November 27, 1863. It appears as a letter sent to higher military authority by a St. Louis law firm hired by Mrs. Musgrave. Unfortunately, the letter has faded so badly over the years in storage that major sections of the letter are unreadable. The letter appears to be an attempt to put the actions of Francis Musgrave into the best possible explanation in a quest for mercy. The next entry in the case record was another letter also dated November 27, 1863, St. Louis, Missouri, and this letter remains very clear. The letter is addressed "*To his Excellency, A. Lincoln, President of United States.*"

The letter begins by saying:

Dear Sir,

My husband, F. M. Musgrave of Pulaski County, Mo. is now confined in Gratiot Prison in this city, awaiting the execution of sentence haped (sic) upon him by Mil[itary] Com[mission], and I am informed by Maj. Dunn, Judge Advocate of the Dept of the Mo. through my attorneys, that the case has been refered (sic)to your excellency for approval, or mitigation of sentence. Allow me to most earnestly implore pardon for my young & misguided husband, whom I am satisfied, if he is restored to liberty, will deport himself hereafter as a good and loyal citizen. He is not a bad man and was frightened away from his home in July 1862, and induced to go south by false and pernicious representations my statement of which to the Provost Marshall General of this Department is herewith presented with official endorsements upon it.

Hoping that you may grant the prayer of your humble petitioner I am your Excellency's most humble servant,

Columbia Musgrave

St Louis Nov. 27th 1863.
To his Excellency, A. Lincoln
President of United States.
Dear Sir
My husband,
F. M. Musgrave, of Pulaski Co.
Mo. is now confined in Gratiot
Prison in this city, awaiting
the execution of sentence
passed upon him by Mil.
Com. And I am informed
by Maj. Dunne, Judge Advocate
of the Dept. of the Mo. through my
attorneys, that the case has
been referred to your excellency
for approval, or mitigation of
sentence. Allow me to most
earnestly implore pardon for my young
& misguided husband, whom I
am satisfied, if he is restored
to liberty, will deport himself

THIS IS THE PART OF THE LETTER OF APPEAL WRITTEN BY COLUMBIA MUSGRAVE "TO HIS EXCELLENCY, A. LINCOLN" IN A DESPERATE ATTEMPT TO SAVE HER HUSBAND'S LIFE.

The stage was then set for the next to last step in the military judicial process. The Judge Advocate General of the United States of America, Joseph Holt, reviewed the case. Holt sent the review to President Lincoln for the final act. Holt's summary of the case follows:

> *Judge Advocate General's Office*
> *August 27, 1863*
> *In the within case, Francis M. Musgrave was charged with violating his oath of allegiance. In that after having taken the oath and bound himself to support, protect, and defend the Government of the United States, he enlisted in a company of Rebels — was sworn into the service of the so-called Confederate States and served in their army for the period of about four months. No testimony was offered by either the prosecution or the defense. The accused plead guilty and stated that he had violated his oath as alleged — that he was a sympathizer with the south and had relatives in the Rebel Army, that he did not want to fight against them. That he served in the Rebel Army for six months but that he was in no battles or skirmishes — that he voluntarily surrendered himself to the Federal Troops — that he wanted to take the oath of allegiance again. The court sentenced him to be shot. General Schofield recommends that the sentence be commuted to confinement in a military prison during the war.*

In the last paragraph, Holt makes reference to General Schofield. Union General John M. Schofield was the Commanding Officer of the Department of Missouri for most of 1863. He was also the General Officer who signed the order appointing the military commission that tried Musgrave. As such higher authority, he had the chance to add his opinion that Musgrave's death sentence should be commuted to time served during the war before the case went to Judge Holt's office in Washington, D.C. for review.

The end of 1863 and start of 1864 were months of critical importance in Civil War fighting. Probably as a result of the extreme demands on his time, President Lincoln did not act on the Musgrave case until early 1864. When he did act, President Lincoln's decision was brief, but very decisive for the defendant and his family.

The last sentence in the case file reads as follows:

Recommendation of General Schofield approved and ordered, February 10, 1864.

A. Lincoln

Judge Advocate General's Office
August 27th 1863

In the within case, Francis M. Musgrave was charged with violating his oath of allegiance. In that after having taken the oath, and bound himself to support, protect, and defend the Government of the United States, he enlisted in a Company of Rebels — was sworn into the service of the so called Confederate States, and served in their Army for the period of about 4 months.

No testimony was offered by either the prosecution or defence. The accused plead guilty and stated that he violated his oath as alleged — that he was a sympathizer with the South, and had relatives in the Rebel Army, that he did not want to fight against them. That he served in the Rebel Army six months & that he was in no battles or skirmishes — that he voluntarily surrendered himself to the Federal troops — that he solicited to take the oath of allegiance again.

The Court sentenced him to be shot. General Schofield recommends that the sentence be commuted to confinement in a military prison during the war.

J. Holt
Judge Adv. General

To the President of the U.S.

Recommendation of General Schofield approved and ordered.
Feb. 10, 1864.
A. Lincoln

President Abraham Lincoln did review the case of Francis M. Musgrave, "a citizen of Pulaski County, Missouri," and commuted his death sentence.

Chapter 4

The Chicken Case

During the Civil War, the city of Rolla, Missouri was a vital target for both sides. The Union Army held the town on the defense, and the Confederates wanted to destroy the town. In many respects the balance of power in southern Missouri went to whomever held the city.

The reason was the railroad. At the start of the war, the westbound expansion of the railroad stopped at Rolla — the end of the tracks for all trains during the war. As such, Rolla automatically became a massive Union Army supply depot for the occupation troops. It was child's play to ship vast quantities of supplies and troops to Rolla by train.

Since every minor town and tavern west of Rolla seemed to have a small Union Army garrison camped there to protect it from the constant raids by southern forces, the supply situation for the Union Army was critical. The ease of supply delivery to Rolla was balanced by the heavy labor needed to supply the small units throughout southern Missouri.

Almost every day of the war some form of teamster wagon delivery started west from Rolla under the guard of Union Cavalry troops. Despite the best efforts of experienced teamsters there was a practical limit to how many miles they could push their teams each day. Thus, supply to areas like Springfield, Missouri could take many days of travel.

During 1861 and 1862, the looming Confederate presence to the south of Rolla prompted the Union Army to plan for a strong defense of Rolla. A series of forts were built to defend Rolla, and tens of thousands of troops were assigned to duty at Rolla. Over a period of the four years of war, with thousands of troops assigned to the town, it was a sure bet that somebody would mess up and get his name before a military court. This chapter covers the story of Private Frank Jones and Private Edward Eastman, who managed to sneak out of camp one night in search of chickens. They found disaster.

The evening of September 12, 1864, the military authorities at Rolla were notified of an attempted robbery near the town. The investigation that followed led to the court martial of Pvt. Eastman. Pvt. Jones was not sent before the court, his fate was much more dramatic.

The charge against Eastman was that he committed the violation of "deserting his colors to pillage and plunder, in violation of the 52nd article of war." According to the first trial specification:

> *On or about the second day of September 1864, in the company of Frank Jones, a private of the same company, in the night time and without the permission of his commanding officer, did leave the camp and colors and in citizen's clothing proceed to a certain place called Diebels farm, and there by force of arms did plunder, pillage, and rob one Phillip Sommerlot, citizen, of one pocket book and sundry articles of clothing and jewelry valued at sixty dollars.*

Specification number two had the same words up to "and in citizen's dress proceed to a certain place called Diebels farm, and there by force of arms did plunder, pillage and rob Mrs. Nancy L. Davis of one revolver valued at thirty dollars. This near Rolla, on or about the second day of September A.D. 1864."

Specification number three followed the same path of wording, but there were a few critical changes. Once again Pvt. Eastman left the camp without permission, in the night, in citizen's dress. He then:

> *...did proceed to the home of Thomas Cole, citizen, and there by force of arms to attempt to possess himself of some arms belonging to said Cole. This near Rolla, Missouri, on or about the twelfth day of September A.D. 1864.*

In this third specification, the date was given as September 12 and not September 2. Also note that the charge said, "attempt to possess by force of arms." And last, the victim's name was given as Thomas Cole.

Answer. In the vicinity of Rolla within two or three miles of the post.

Ques. J.A. Did anything further in regard to this case, come to your knowledge, regarding the prisoner state what it was.

Answer I was sent over by Genl. McNeil to take the testimony of the man who was shot and who was not expected to live, I found him at the Hospital very low, the surgeon had announced to him, that he could not live, and it was with difficulty that he could speak, he was evidently fast sinking.

Ques. J.A. Was he aware that he was on the point of death,

Answer Yes he was.

Ques. J.A. State what he said in regard to the prisoner.

Answer He said that he and Eastman went out that night into the country. he stated his object was to buy chickens, they stopped at this house at about half after nine O'clock. for some water, that they were invited in, that he went into the house and Eastman stood at the door, with his revolver drawn, that they got the water, and Eastman asked the man

A SAMPLE PAGE OF THE TRIAL RECORD FROM THE CASE OF PRIVATE EDWARD EASTMAN, THE SOLDIER WHO WAS ACCUSED OF "DESERTING HIS COLORS TO PILLAGE AND PLUNDER, IN VIOLATION OF THE 52ND ARTICLE OF WAR."

Following the reading of the charge and specifications, Private Eastman was asked for his formal plea. Eastman entered a guilty plea to the first two specifications. He entered a not guilty plea to the third specification. With his plea of guilty to the first two specifications involving armed robbery and pillage, Private Eastman was assured of some type of punishment from the court-martial board. In these first two cases of armed robbery, nobody was hurt. In the robbery attempt on Cole things had not gone well for the prisoner and his partner, Private Frank Jones.

The court then moved to trial on specification number three by calling the first witness. Thomas Cole was called to the stand and duly sworn to tell the truth. Cole stated he was a farmer and lived "about three and one-half miles southeast from Rolla." He also testified that on September 12, 1864, he was at his home. Following a few more minor questions, Cole moved into the important part of his testimony.

The exact question and answer sequence follows:

Q: Did anything particular happen at your house that night? State all that happened.

A: About ten o'clock on Monday night the twelfth, I believe, two men came to my house and knocked on the door. I asked who was there, and they said, 'a friend.' I told them I wanted to know who that friend was, and one of them said it was Thomas. I asked them what they wanted. They said they wanted a drink of water, and I got them some water, took it to the door, and gave it to him. I asked the other one whether he wanted any, and he said 'no.' Then the other one behind asked me if I was a soldier. I told him no. He then asked whether I was a teamster. I told him I was not. He asked my name and I gave it, he then asked me whether I had any firearms. I told him I had. He said they wanted them. I told him they could not have them. At that, the forward one cocked his revolver, and I stepped around to the door and shot him, and then they both ran off.

Q: Which one of the two told you that he wanted your firearms, the one you shot or the other one?

A: The one I did not shoot.

Q: Are you very positive that you never saw the prisoner before? Look at him close.

A: He resembles the man, but I could not swear positive that he is the man. It was too dark and his face was so close to the shade that I could not identify him.

Q: Was the man you did not shoot at armed at the time?

A: I could not swear that he was.

Q: Did you ever see any of these men again afterwards?

A: I saw the one I shot afterwards about three hours. He came back and laid on my bed, one of the scouts that came out asked him his name. He told me his name was Jones, and he was a Union soldier. I asked him what he cocked his revolver for, and he made no answer at all.

The witness was then dismissed and a second witness was called to the stand. This witness had some interesting things to say:

Q: State your name, occupation and residence.

A: My name is William R. Strachan. I am a Special Agent of the United States Secret Police; was ordered to report here to General McNeil, on special service.

Q: Do you know the prisoner?

A: I do. That is to say I helped to examine him, I never saw him before that time.

Q: On what particular occasion did you examine him?

A: He was arrested on a charge of marauding and pilfering in the neighborhood.

Q: Did you have any conversation with the prisoner at that time, and what was the main feature of it?

A: The prisoner confessed to me that he was out with the man who was shot, on two occasions, that he was out with him the night he was shot. He not only confessed that, but he also gave me the particulars of the conversation.

Q: State what the particulars were.

A: He said the other man had impositioned him to go out with him, and they changed their clothes, and they made quite a round and started back to town. When they stopped at this house for some water. Said they got the water, he asked the man of the house one or two questions, one was whether the man was armed, when he asked him that question, that the man fired and shot his comrade. He went off with his comrade a piece, bandaged his wound, and while he was attending him, he told his comrade that he would leave him, and he started for his quarters. That is the substance of his statement in this transaction.

Q: Did he tell you at whose house this happened?

A: No, except that it was at the house where his comrade was shot.

Q: Do you know the name of the man who was shot?

A: His reported name is Frank Jones.

Q: When was it the prisoner made this confession to you?

A: It was on the same day that Frank died, either on the thirteenth or the fourteenth of this month.

Q: Do you know where all the prisoner stated to you did happen?

A: In the vicinity of Rolla, within two or three miles of the post.

Q: Did anything further in regard to this case, come to your knowledge regarding the prisoner? State what it was.

A: I was sent over by General McNeil to take the testimony of the man who was shot and who was not expected to live. I found him at the hospital, pretty low. The surgeon had announced to him that he could not live, and it was with difficulty that he could speak. He was evidently fast sinking.

Q: Was he aware that he was on the point of death?

A: Yes, he was.

Q: State what he said in regard to the prisoner.

[Author's note: In a court of law, the testimony you give must be direct, that is you saw or heard the defendant take some action. You can't testify that Joe told you Pete did the crime. This is the hearsay rule of evidence. But there is one major exception to the rule, the 'dying declaration.' This exception allows the final words of someone with knowledge of the case to be presented into the court by a second person. The legal requirement that must be shown before the testimony is allowed is that the person did know he was going to die, and did in fact die. This requirement accounts for the past few questions in the transcript. Once the legal requirement is proven, the person's final words are allowed to stand.]

A: He said that he and Eastman went out that night into the county. He stated his object was to buy chickens. They stopped at this house at about half after nine o'clock for some water. That they were invited into the house, and Eastman stood at the door with his revolver drawn, that they got the water, and Eastman asked the man if he was a teamster, or if he was a soldier, the man said no, that Eastman then asked him if he had any arms, and as this was asked the man made a spring to one side, and fired and shot him. He, Jones was setting down at the time that Eastman ran off. That he went out of the house into the brush and laid down, that he got up and came back into the house and found none there. He threw himself onto the bed, where he was when they came out after him. It was with great difficulty in speech he gave this testimony, He was holding his hand to his wound during all the time.

The next witness to speak was 2nd Lieutenant Thomas Davis, Battery B, 2nd Missouri Light Artillery Volunteers. 2LT Davis was Private Eastman's immediate superior officer. Davis gave the court several more parts of the total story.

Q: Where were you on or about the twelfth day of September, 1864?

A: I was here in camp near Rolla.

Q: Did anything unusual happen in your camp about that day?

A: About one o'clock on the morning of the thirteenth, I was awakened at night by the men of the Fifth Missouri State Militia Cavalry. I believe they belonged to the Fifth. He told me a man of our battery was wounded out on the Salem road. He also told me the man's name was Jones. I went up to Fort Wyman and got an ambulance from Doctor Johnson, and went to the house where he was. The place I judge to be between three and four miles from base. When I got there, I found the place guarded by a squad of cavalry. I went in and found a man by name of Jones, lying on a bed on the floor, mortally wounded. I put him in the ambulance and brought him to the post hospital at Rolla.

Q: What became of that man afterward?

A: I received notice that the man died about ten o'clock a.m. the next morning of the thirteenth.

Q: In which direction from Rolla was the house situated, where you found Jones?

A: About southeast from here.

Q: Do you know the prisoner?

A: Yes, his name is Edward Eastman.

At this point the prosecution had no further questions for 2LT Davis and turned him over to Private Eastman for any defense questions. Eastman had no questions, but a member of the Court-martial board did have some questions to ask.

Q: Was the prisoner in camp that night?

A: He was present at retreat, on Monday the twelfth and I did not see him afterward until noon next day, in the camp guardhouse.

Q: What was he put in the guardhouse for?

A: I don't know.

Q: What was the general character of the prisoner since he has been in the company?

A: He has been wild and reckless.

Q: How long did he serve in your company?

A: I think he was enlisted in the early part of June 1864, at Springfield.

The members of the Military Court-martial Board had no more questions, and LT Davis was dismissed from the witness stand. At this point the Judge Advocate announced he had presented his case and had no more witnesses to call.

The transcript record shows that the prisoner had no witness to introduce on the part of the defense. However, the prisoner here stated orally to the court that he was:

...coerced into it, and never done anything of that sort until this time, this being my first freak [Author's note: the transcript was quite clear he did use the word freak. I don't know how to interpret his use of the word.] I hope the court will be as easy with me as possible, and I will try to be a good soldier.

Eastman then submitted the case to the court without further remark.

The court was then cleared for deliberation and having maturely considered the evidence adduced find the prisoner, Edward Eastman, Private of Company B, Second Missouri Light Artillery as follows:

Of the First Specification, Guilty

Of the Second Specification, Guilty

Of the Third Specification, Guilty

Of the Charge, Guilty

And the Court does therefore sentence him, Private Edward Eastman of Company B, Second Missouri Light Artillery, that he be shot to death with musketry at such time and place as the General Commanding may direct, two thirds of the members concurring therein.

The death sentence was sent to a higher authority for review. On September 17, 1864, General McNeil, Commanding the District of Rolla wrote:

Proceeding, findings, and sentence approved.

The case was then sent to William S. Rosecrans, Commanding General, Department of Missouri. General Rosecrans added a memo to the case file on September 21, 1864, from his headquarters in St. Louis, Missouri.

The memo stated:

Finding and sentence confirmed. The sentence will be carried into effect on the 7th Day of October 1864, under the direction of the Commanding Officer of the District of Rolla, Missouri. In confirming the just sentence in this case, the General Commanding desires to warn all soldiers in his command of the stern punishment prescribed for offenses of this class, and of his determination to prevent their occurrence in the future, by vigorous enforcement of the rigors of the law.

E | 2 L. Art'y. | Mo.

Edward Eastman

Pvt., 3d Battery B, 2 Reg't Missouri L. Art'y.

Appears on

Battery Muster Roll

for Nov. & Dec., 1864.

Present or absent Absent.

Stoppage, $ .... 100 for ....

Due Gov't, $ .... 100 for ....

Valuation of horse, $ 100

Valuation of horse equipments, $ 100

Remarks: Rec'd $13 - adv. pay & $25 bounty. In confinement at Rolla Mo.

Book mark: ....

(358) C. S. Clark Copyist.

E | 2 L. Art'y. | Mo.

Edward Eastman

Pvt., 3d Battery B, 2 Reg't Missouri L. Art'y.

Appears on

Battery Muster Roll

for July & Aug., 1864.

Present or absent Present.

Stoppage, $ .... 100 for ....

Due Gov't, $ .... 100 for ....

Valuation of horse, $ 100

Valuation of horse equipments, $ 100

Remarks: Rec'd $13 advance pay & $25 bounty.

Book mark: ....

(358) Lowry Copyist.

These Battery Muster Roll cards kept by the Union Army on Private Eastman reveals that he was given $13.00 pay advance, and a $25.00 bounty for his enlistment, and further shows that he is absent from his unit, and that he's held in confinement at Rolla, Missouri.

The thoughts of Pvt. Eastman as he sat in the Guard House waiting for October 7th to arrive were not recorded. However, he probably greeted the next entry in the file with a shout of joy. On October 5th, the following order was issued:

> *The execution of the sentence of death in the case of Edward Eastman, Co. B, 2nd Artillery Missouri Volunteers, as promulgated in Department Orders No. 174, current series, from these Headquarters is suspended until further orders.*

The suspension order was signed by General Rosecrans. The case file doesn't give any reason why the execution was suspended. In our modern world, such a stay of execution could take years to run the appeals course. In this Civil War case, it only took twenty days.

On October 25, 1864, Headquarters Department of the Missouri, in St. Louis, Missouri issued Special Order No. 296 which read as follows:

> *The sentence of death in the case of Edward Eastman, promulgated in General Orders No. 174 (cs) from these Headquarters, will be carried into effect on the 25th Day of November 1864 as directed in said orders.*

Once again General Rosecrans signed the order. The case file doesn't contain a description of the events of November 25th at Rolla, however a number of official notes on military documents contained in the Army personnel file of Edward Eastman make it quite certain that the death sentence was carried out as ordered.

Head Quarters, Department of the Missouri,

St. Louis Mo. Oct 25 1864

SPECIAL ORDERS,
No 296

EXTRACT.

2. . . The sentence of death in the case of Edward Eastman, promulgated in General Orders No 174 (C.S) from these Head Quarters will be carried into effect on the 25th day of Nov. 1864 as directed in said orders

By Command of Major General Rosecrans,

[illegible]
Assistant Adjutant General.

SPECIAL ORDERS NO. 296 — THE SENTENCE OF DEATH IN THE CASE OF PRIVATE EDWARD EASTMAN ON THE 25TH DAY OF NOVEMBER, 1864 AS DIRECTED BY THE COURT.

[Author's note: During this trial, testimony was heard from a William R. Strachan, a Special Agent of the United States Secret Police. I'm not exactly sure just what the title he used means, but I thought it interesting that one W. R. Strachan was referred to in another case as a Deputy United States Marshall. This reference is in the *Official Records*, Series 2, Vol. 1, page 207. In this case, Strachan had made an arrest here in Missouri and brought the suspect to the military. I should also mention that during the Civil War, the United States Government did frequently execute Union military members. Depending on which source you read the number varies, but many sources agree that the correct number is about two hundred sixty-seven men.]

DEATH AND DISABILITY RECORDS.

Edward Eastman, Pvt.
Co. B. 2 Art. Mo. - Shot for
the offense of Desertion and
pillage, Nov. 25, 1864. - G.O.,
No. 174. Dept. of the Missouri,
Sept. 23, 1864. — See List
of U. S. soldiers executed by
U. S. military authorities
Pages 4 & 6.
See 5981. A. - A. G. O.
(E. B.) Aug. 7-85
W. S. B. 10-2-85

A DOCUMENT FROM GOVERNMENT FILES THAT CONFIRMS THE FIRING SQUAD DID THEIR DUTY AND CARRIED OUT THE EXECUTION OF PRIVATE EASTMAN.

E	2 L. Art'y.	Mo.

Edward Eastman

Privt, 3d Battery B, 2 Reg't Mo. Lt. Art'y.

Age 19 years.

Appears on **Batt'y Muster-out Roll,** dated

St. Louis Mo, Dec 20, 1865.

Muster-out to date ...., 186 .

Last paid to ...., 186 .

Clothing account:

Last settled Never, 186 ; drawn since $......100

Due soldier $.........100; due U. S. $.........100

Am't for cloth'g in kind or money adv'd $ 67 78/100

Due U. S. for arms, equipments, &c., $.........100

Bounty paid $ 25 100; due $ 75 100

Valuation of horse, $.........100

Valuation of horse equipments, $.........100

Remarks: Died - Executed by military Authorities at Rolla Mo. Nov 25th 64

Book mark: ....

B. F. Evans
Copyist.

(361)

E	2 L. Art'y.	Mo.

Edward Eastman

Pvt., 3d Battery B, 2 Reg't Missouri L. Art'y.

Appears on

Battery Muster Roll

for Jany & Feby, 1865.

Present or absent ....

Stoppage, $.........100 for ....

Due Gov't, $.........100 for ....

Valuation of horse, $.........100

Valuation of horse equipments, $.........100

Remarks: Died. Rec'd $13 - adv. pay & $25 - bounty executed by the military authorities at Rolla Mo Nov. 25/64.

Book mark: ....

(358)

O. J. Clark
Copyist.

Closing the record on Private Eastman, the Battery Muster-Out Roll, which shows that Edward "Died — Executed by Military Authorities at Rolla, Mo. Nov 25th 64" at the age of 19.

Adjutant General's Office.

Washington, Mch. 9, 1868

[MEMORANDUM FOR OFFICE USE]

It appears from the Rolls on file in this Office, that Edw. Eastman was enrolled on the 31 day of May, 1864, at Springfield, Mo. for Company B, 2 Regiment of Mo. Art. Volunteers, to serve 3 years, or during the war, and mustered into service as a Private on the 1 day of June, 1864, at Springfield, Mo. in Company B, 2 Regiment of Mo. Art. Volunteers, to serve 3 years, or during the war. On the Muster Roll of Company B, of that Regiment, for the months of Jany & Feb, 1865, he is reported "Executed by the Military authorities at Rolla, Mo., Nov. 25, 1864."

Edw. D. Beck[?]

A. A. Genl.

J.W.K.

THE ADJUTANT GENERAL'S FINAL DISPOSITION OF PRIVATE EDWARD EASTMAN.

Chapter 5

Murder at Breakfast

The next trial concerns a case of murder committed in the state of Missouri, however, the trial was held on board a Union ship in the waters off the coast of Louisiana. The Army command involved in the case had been in Missouri but was suddenly transferred to duty in Louisiana. When you check the dates involved in the murder and the trial, you'll find that the Union Army covered a lot of ground in a short period of time. It appears they moved a full division of infantry from Missouri to Louisiana in just about sixty-two days, or maybe a little less.

The murder occurred on May 28, 1863. The division moved out one or two weeks later for Louisiana, and the trial board was convened July 31. In view of the transportation methods available during the Civil War, this troop movement appears to be a pretty impressive achievement by the Union Army.

The court-martial of Pvt. John Campbell began on board the steamer, *Tecumseh*, off Port Hudson, Louisiana on July 31,1863, at nine o'clock a.m.

> *The court then proceeded with the trial of Private John Campbell, Company D, Twenty-sixth Indiana Volunteer Infantry, who was called before the court and having heard the order read appointing the court was asked if he had any objection to any member named in the order. To which the accused replied that he had none.*
>
> *The court was then in the presence of the accused, duly sworn by the Judge Advocate, and the Judge Advocate was duly sworn by the President of the Court. The accused was*

then asked if he had or desired counsel to assist him in his defense, to which he replied that he did not.

Whereupon the accused, Private John Campbell, Company D, Twenty-sixth Regiment Indiana Volunteer Infantry was duly arraigned on the following charges and specification. To wit: Charge, Murder. Specification: In this, that said Private John Campbell of Company D, Twenty-sixth Indiana Volunteer Infantry, did willfully and feloniously and with malice aforethought, kill one Moses H. Hughes, Private, Company D, Twenty-sixth Regiment, Indiana Volunteer Infantry, all this at Camp Herron, near Pilot Knob, state of Missouri, on or about the twenty-eighth day A.D. 1863.

To which charge and specification, the accused pleaded as follows, namely, to the specification, not guilty. To the charge, not guilty.

At this point the actual trial began with the first testimony.

Private Charles B. Matthews, a witness for the prosecution was then duly sworn and testified as follows:

Q: What is your name, age, rank, and to what command do you belong?

A: My name is Charles B. Matthews, age nineteen years, Private Company D, Twenty-sixth Indiana Volunteer Infantry.

Q: Where were you on or about the twenty-eighth day of May last?

A: I think I was in Pilot Knob, Missouri.

Q: Do you know the accused, Private John Campbell Company D, Twenty-sixth Indiana Volunteer Infantry?

A: I am not personally acquainted with him, that is not intimately. I belong to the same company, and have a passing acquaintance with him.

Q: Did the accused and Private Moses H. Hughes of the same company have difficulty about Twenty-eighth May last? If so, state all you know about it and what was done by accused.

A: I know of no difficulty between them except that Campbell shot Hughes.

Q: State all you know about the circumstances of accused shooting Hughes.

A: Well, one morning we were at breakfast and Hughes and myself were sitting down there together, and the accused came out and called me, and told me to come away from there. He wanted to see me. I went up to him, and he told me not to talk to that man. I turned around and was going to go back when I heard the click of a gun, and I turned around again and I saw the gun up to the accused's face. At the same instant, the gun was fired, and Hughes fell. That is about all I know, except the orderly came around and arrested the accused.

Q: Who fired the gun, and who was it fired at?

A: The gun was fired by the accused, and it was pointed at Hughes. The ball hit Hughes.

Q: Where did the ball hit Hughes?

A: It went into his head about a full inch above, and a little back of his right eye and came out just above his left ear.

Q: What effect did the shot have — did it kill him, and if so how long did he live after he was shot?

A: It killed him instantly.

Q: What kind of gun did accused have, and what kind and size ball did it carry?

A: It was an Enfield Rifle. Do not know what the size, it carried a cone shaped ball.

Q: Was the ball found that passed through Hughes head, and did you see it?

A: Do not know whether it was found or not.

Q: What did accused say to Hughes, if anything, just prior to shooting him?

A: Did not hear him say a word.

Q: How long after you first saw accused that morning, was it before he shot Hughes?

A: I suppose it was an hour and a half from the time I first saw him — I saw him before breakfast.

Q: How long was it after you first saw the gun in accused hands, before he shot Hughes?

A: I did not see him have a gun at all. I heard a click, and turned around and looked and saw a gun in his hands and leveled at Hughes. I saw a gun standing by the tent right opposite of him. Do not know if it was his gun.

Q: Did he have a gun in his hand when he called you as above stated?

A: No Sir.

Q: Where did this shooting happen?

A: At Pilot Knob, Missouri, at quarters of Company. D Twenty-sixth Indiana Volunteers.

Q: Can you tell me about the day of the month, what number and what year it was?

A: It was in the year 1863, don't recollect the number or the day of the month.

Q: Do you know how many days it was prior to your regiment leaving Pilot Knob, Missouri?

A: Do not, it was about a week or more.

Q: What company and regiment did Hughes belong to, and what was his rank?

A: He was a private, and belonged to Company D, Twenty-sixth Indiana Volunteer Infantry.

Q: Did you hear any conversation between Hughes and accused within a day or two of the shooting of Hughes?

A: Did not hear them have any quarrel, or high words, or any fuss.

Q: Do you know from what you heard Hughes or accused say, or from your own personal knowledge in any way, why accused shot Hughes?

A: No Sir, I do not.

Q: What did accused do immediately after shooting Hughes, and what did he say about it, if anything?

A: He just set his gun down on the ground, and looked rather wild at Hughes. The orderly came up then and took him to the guardhouse. He said something, but I did not hear it. I have no idea what he said.

Q: How did accused look when he called you away from Hughes, excited and wild or natural?

A: He looked natural — did not look excited at all.

Q: Do you know whether accused had been drinking that morning?

A: I could not say — I do not know.

At this point the prosecution had no more questions for Pvt. Matthews. The accused did not ask any questions in his defense and the members of the court did not have any parts of his testimony they wanted to question. The trial moved to the next witness.

Q: What is your name, age, rank, and to what command do you belong?

A: My name is John S. Hadley, age twenty-eight years. Private Company D, Twenty-sixth Indiana Volunteers.

Q: Are you acquainted with John Campbell, the accused?

A: Yes, Sir.

Q: Were you acquainted with one Moses H. Hughes of Company D, Twenty-sixth Indiana Volunteers?

A: Yes, Sir.

Q: State if you know anything of the accused shooting any person about May last. If so, state who he shot, when and where it was, and state particularly the details how it occurred.

A: At Camp Herron, near Pilot Knob State of Missouri on the twenty-eighth day of May last, we were eating breakfast and Campbell called Matthews to him. I did not hear what passed between them. I looked up in a minute afterward and saw Campbell have a gun in his hand. I did not see him shoot it — I heard a gun crack, and saw Hughes fall over. Hughes at the time was sitting on one side of the fire and I on the other. Hughes fell with his head pretty near with the fire, and Tracy, I think, pulled him out. The orderly Sergeant came down and took what Hughes had in his pockets out, and the boys carried him and washed him off.

Q: Do you know who fired the gun at Hughes?

A: I do not. I could not say.

Q: Did you see accused immediately after Hughes was shot — and what was he doing and what did he have in his hand?

A: He was pulling the hammer back and blowing down the muzzle of a gun he had in his hand, and then set the gun down against the tent.

Q: How far off was accused from Hughes, when Hughes was shot?

A: He might have been twenty or thirty feet, I could not say exactly.

Q: Did you hear Hughes say anything after he was shot?

A: No, Sir.

Q: Where was he shot, and how long did he live afterwards?

A: He was shot in the right side of the forehead and the ball came out above his ear on the left side. He died instantly after being shot.

Q: How loud was the report of the gun — as loud as an ordinary cartridge would make it?

A: Think the report was not as loud as an ordinary cartridge would make it.

Q: Did you hear the accused say anything immediately after the shooting? If so, what?

A: He came up after his blankets from the guardhouse and said to me, 'I expect some of the boys think I have played hell this morning.'

Q: Did you hear the accused say anything to Hughes, just before he was shot?

A: I did not, Sir.

Q: How long after the shooting before you heard the above remark from accused?

A: Do not know how long. I had been up to the Doctor's and got a little medicine. It might have been an hour, or a little more or a little less.

Q: How did accused look, and what did he say after the shooting before the Sergeant took him to the guardhouse?

A: He looked a little wild when the Sergeant was taking him to the guardhouse. He said something to the Sergeant, but I don't know what it was.

Q: Do you know what property or money the Sergeant found on the person of Hughes?

A: I do not, Sir.

Q: Do you know from your own knowledge, or from anything you heard Hughes or the accused say previous to the shooting, why accused shot Hughes? If so, state.

A: Campbell told me that morning before the shooting that he was going to kill the damned son of a bitch — he had stolen his money once before — a two-dollar bill he had marked and knew he had stolen it from him.

Q: How did this conversation begin?

A: I was standing there talking to Thomas Roark, and Campbell came up and said as I have above stated.

Q: Did you understand who he referred to when he said he would kill the damned son of a bitch?

A: I did not — I thought he was gassing, as he generally was after he had been on a spree.

Q: Was the accused drunk or sober when this conversation took place?

A: I don't suppose he was exactly sober. He came in the night before with a canteen of whiskey, pretty drunk.

Q: How long after this conversation, before Hughes was shot?

A: It might have been an hour or more.

Q: Did you ever know of accused and Hughes having any difficulty? If so what was it about?

A: I do not know of them ever having any difficulty.

The prosecution then turned the witness over to the defense. With neither the accused nor the court having any questions for him, the witness was then dismissed from the stand. The next witness was then called and sworn.

Q: What is your name, age, rank, and to what command do you belong?

A: My name is Dennis Tracy, age eighteen years, am Private in Company D, Twenty-sixth Indiana Volunteer Infantry.

Q: Are you acquainted with the accused, and how long have you known him?

A: I am acquainted with him somewhat. Have been in the same company with him two years.

Q: State all you know if anything, about accused shooting one Moses H. Hughes, Private Company D, Twenty-sixth Indiana Volunteers about twenty-eighth May last.

A: On the night of the twenty-seventh May last, John Campbell was walking in front of his company's tents, and was swearing that someone had drugged his whiskey and stolen his money, and he swore at the same time that the man that stole it had received a furlough but it would not do him any good. I heard nothing more until about six o'clock next morning when I heard Campbell say he would shoot the son of a bitch — he did not name anyone — at the same time Hughes stepped out of his tent with his gun, as he was going to roll-call, and asked Campbell if he meant him. Campbell said he did not accuse any man, but the one that had his money — not naming who he was. Did not hear any name 'til about seven o'clock — it might have been a quarter past seven — the mess was eating breakfast when Campbell called Private Matthews to him and said something to him, but I did not hear what it was. At this same time, I passed between Campbell and Hughes and went to the right about thirty feet. Hughes was setting in front of the fire, eating his breakfast. I saw Campbell raise his gun and fire, and Hughes fell over; his head pretty near into the fire. The ball went in at the right side of his forehead and came out above his left ear. After Campbell had shot him, he cocked his gun and blew into the muzzle of it, and then laid the gun up against the tent and walked up towards Captain Wallace's quarters, to the head of the company, where he met Sergeant Robinson and told him he had killed one son of a bitch, and the Sergeant put him under arrest and took him down to the guardhouse.

Q: Did you ever hear any conversation between Hughes and the accused other than you have above stated about stealing accused money?

A: I did not.

Q: Did you hear accused say anything immediately after he shot Hughes and before he spoke to the Sergeant? If so, what?

A: No, Sir, I did not hear him say anything.

Q: Was the accused drunk or sober when he shot Hughes?

A: I do not believe he was sober, and I do not believe he was drunk either. He had been drinking the night before.

Q: Do you know whether he had been drinking for several days prior to this time?

A: I do not.

Q: Was the accused in the habit of drinking to excess, prior to the shooting of Hughes?

A: He was, whenever he could get liquor.

Q: What opportunity had he had for getting liquor for a month or so before the shooting?

A: He had very good opportunity, as we were at St. Louis, Missouri.

Q: Do you know whether the accused had delirium tremors about the time, or shortly before the shooting?

A: I do not.

Q: Had he drank liquor pretty steadily and in large quantities for a month or so before the shooting?

A: I believe he had.

Q: Do you know what property or money or both Hughes had on his person when shot?

A: No, Sir.

Neither the accused or the court having any questions to ask the witness, he was discharged for the present. Here the court postponed the further consideration of this case until tomorrow morning at eight o'clock.

When the court met the following morning, in a surprise move the prosecution rested their case against Campbell. The accused was asked if he had any witnesses to present to the court.

The accused then introduced the following witness in his behalf, Marmanduke L. Robbins, who being first duly sworn testifies as follows:

The questions in the following testimony are now asked by the accused.

Q: What is your name, rank, and to what command do you belong.

A: My name is Marmanduke L. Robbins, age thirty-two years, Private Company D, Twenty-sixth Indiana Volunteer Infantry.

Q: Are you acquainted with the accused, and did you also know Moses H. Hughes when living?

A: I know both of them well.

Q: Do you know by what you have heard accused say as to why he shot Hughes?

Here the Court was cleared, and the Judge Advocate objected to the court about the nature of the defense questions by the accused, and the court decided that although the testimony was not legal, [Author's note: they refer to the hearsay rule of evidence] yet in mercy, it will listen to testimony the accused may offer in justification of his acts. The court was then opened, the accused party and witness present when the witness answered the questions as follows:

Q: Do you know anything of Hughes stealing money from Campbell of your own knowledge?

A: Hughes had boasted to me one time before that he had stolen money from the accused.

Q: State when this was and how much money Hughes said he stole from accused, and when he stole it. Give all the particulars.

A: Well, as for the date I could not give it. It was at Camp Totten, Missouri. Hughes had went out to Rolla and by some means or other had got hold of a watch, and I asked him how he came by it, and he told me he had taken it from a citizen. He also took out his pocket book and showed me some money and said he had taken it from Campbell — some eight or nine dollars.

Q: Did he say when or how he had taken the money from Campbell?

A: No, Sir, he did not — he just said he had taken it from Campbell.

Q: Had your regiment been paid off about that time?

A: The regiment had been paid off only a short time before that — not more than a couple of days — if that long.

Q: Do you know of any other time that Hughes took money from the accused?

A: No, Sir, not to my knowledge.

Q: Had accused made any complaint to your knowledge, of having lost money, about the time Hughes told you he had taken his money?

A: Yes, Sir. A short time before Hughes came in from Rolla — they were out there together — accused told me he had lost money and believed Hughes took it.

Q: State what you know, if anything, of Hughes and accused getting drunk, or drinking liquor together and how often — and whether they messed [ate meals] together.

A: They messed together and often drank liquor together.

Q: Do you know anything about their drinking immediately after payday — if so state fully.

A: I can't say — I was not out with them at Rolla. I have known them to drink often and get drunk together just after payday.

Q: How long have you been in the company?

A: Two years and two days now, Sir.

Q: How many times have you heard of accused losing money during the two years?

A: Accused has told me he lost money three times — once at Rolla — once at Springfield — and once at Pilot Knob, Missouri.

Q: Do you know how much he lost at each time?

A: I do not.

Q: Was your regiment paid at the time and place you have named?

A: Yes, Sir, they were.

Q: How long a time was the regiment paid for at each place?

A: At Springfield, we were paid for two or four months — up to about August 1862. Near Rolla, Missouri at Camp Totten we were paid for four months — at Pilot Knob, Missouri, for two months.

Q: Do you know of your regiment being paid at Camp Schofield about February last?

A: I was not there — I was at Fayetteville.

Q: Do you know of accused losing one dollar and a jackknife at St. Louis on the platform when Hughes was with him?

A: Yes, Sir. He lost a dollar and a knife.

Q: Do you know who took it?

A: I saw Hughes with the knife afterwards.

Q: Did you ever hear accused complain that Hughes had stolen it?

A: I believe I heard him say he thought Hughes had stole it.

Q: When the regiment was paid off at Pilot Knob, Missouri, did Hughes give you any money? And, how much?

A: He paid me seven dollars and a half the night he received his money.

Q: How many months was Hughes paid for at Pilot Knob, Missouri?

A: I think he was paid for two months like the rest of us.

Q: Did Hughes have any money, just before he was paid at Pilot Knob?

A: If he did he kept it concealed, for he was trying to borrow among the company — he did borrow about seven dollars and a half from me about two weeks before we were paid off.

Q: Did he use the money he borrowed from you before pay day?

A: I know of his using part of it for a quart of whiskey — that's all I know of his using to my knowledge.

Q: Do you know of his using any money besides what he paid you, after he was paid off?

A: I do not. I know he was on a spree with accused the day before, and I suppose he used some money.

Q: Do you know how much money accused lost at Pilot Knob?

A: I do not.

Q: Did you ever tell accused that Hughes had told you that he had stolen his money at Rolla?

A: I was afraid to for fear he would commit the same act he did at Pilot Knob, Missouri. I know the man well enough to know he would not be run over.

Q: Do you know of accused making any complaints to his company officers, that Hughes stole his money?

A: Not to my knowledge.

Q: Did you ever hear me accuse Hughes of stealing my money, and what did he say?

A: I never heard you accuse Hughes separately. I heard you say to three men and Hughes was one of them, that you believed one of them had your money. Hughes said he would be the last man to steal from as good a man as John Campbell.

Q: Do you know of Hughes and I gambling together at any time?

A: I never knew you to play with Hughes except for sport — I never knew you to gamble since you have been in the company.

At this time the witness was excused from the stand. The next witness was called and sworn to tell the truth.

Q: State your name, age, rank and to what command do you belong.

A: My name is Augustus D. Rose, age thirty-six years, Lieutenant Colonel of the Twenty-sixth Indiana Volunteer Infantry.

Q: Are you acquainted with me, and did you know Moses H. Hughes in his lifetime, and how long have you known me and him?

A: I am well acquainted with both of you, and have known you since July 1861.

Q: Were you Captain of Company D, Twenty-sixth Indiana Volunteers, and if so how long?

A: I was Captain of Company D, Twenty-sixth Indiana Volunteers from its organization in July 1861, until July 1862 and had command of the company two months after July 1862.

Q: What is and has been my character as a soldier and a man since you have known me?

A: Your character as a soldier was always good except you would drink occasionally. You were always prompt to duty and never knew you to grumble at anything you had to do as a soldier. You were always honest and truthful, and whatever you said could be depended on.

Q: What was the character of Hughes as a soldier and as a man?

A: It was rather bad in this way — he would get intoxicated and was hard to manage. When sober, he would grumble. I have had to tie him down when intoxicated.

Q: What was his reputation for honesty among his comrades?

A: His reputation was not good. He was thought to take things that did not belong to him.

Q: State all you know about Hughes having taken money from me, and whether I ever made any complaint that he had stolen my money.

A: Before I left the command of the company, I think you complained twice that your money was taken and by men at your own mess, and at one time you believed Hughes had taken it, and that it was a damned shame that a soldier should have to lose his money by a man in his own mess. Hughes was a member of your mess, the whole time. I told you not to accuse any man openly but to watch for an over amount of money in any man's hands in your mess and I would do the same.

Q: State what effect liquor has upon me, and what effect it had on Hughes.

A: When you drink it has the effect to quiet you — you are a very still man anyway — and a great amount of liquor has the effect to prostrate you and you do not know anything. It had the effect on Hughes to exasperate him — I don't think I ever knew him to drink enough to quiet him. He was always in difficulty and wanted to fight someone when drunk.

The witness was dismissed. The Judge Advocate nor the court having any questions, the accused called Nicholas Evans who being first duly sworn testified as follows:

Q: What is your name, age, rank, and to what command do you belong?

A: My name is Nicholas Evans, age thirty-seven years, Private Company D, Twenty-sixth Indiana Volunteers.

Q: Are you acquainted with me? If so for how long have you known me?

A: I know you, and have known you since July 1861.

Q: Have you been in the same mess with me, and how long?

A: Have been in the same company about eighteen months.

Q: Did you know Moses H. Hughes in his lifetime?

A: Yes, Sir.

Q: Was he in the same mess with me and how long?

A: He was in the same mess since July 1861.

Q: Do you know anything of my losing money at Pilot Knob, Missouri about May last?

A: All I know is you said you had lost about fourteen dollars.

Q: Do you remember the night I said I lost the money?

A: Yes, Sir.

Q: Was I drunk or sober that night?

A: I think you were drinking.

Q: Did you see Hughes that night, and when? What was he doing, and what time of night was it?

A: I saw Hughes after dark awhile around his tent. Don't recollect seeing him after taps.

Q: Did you hear me say anything about losing money the morning I shot Hughes? If so, what?

A: I heard you say in the morning that someone had stolen your money. I heard you say it in the night directly after you missed it. You said in the night when you first woke up that you had been robbed of your money and you believed Hughes had it, as he had robbed you twice before and had been following you all day to get you drunk and get what you had. You talked considerable, I remember all. You said you would give him to morning to find it up and it would be all right and you would let him go, but if he did not find up the money you would give him a furlough that would do him all his time, or something to that effect. Hughes had a furlough then to go home. That was all I heard you say—part of this was said in the night, and part the next morning. I think it was about twelve or one o'clock that night that you missed your money.

ans. Yes: after Huffers was shot I believe you wanted Humphrey served as you thought they were both concerned in the matter - this was while I was taking you to the guard house - you blamed one pretty near as much as the other.

Quest. by ac. What did I say to you that morning while you were taking me to the guard house?

ans. When I first went to you, I asked you if you knew what you had done. You said you had done just what you said you was going to do. I asked you what you thought would be done with you. You said if you had this other man - Humphrey - out of the way, you should be willing to die - you expected to die any way for what you had done.

The Court nor Judge advocate having no further questions, the witness is discharged.

A SAMPLE PAGE OF THE TRIAL TRANSCRIPT FROM THE MURDER CASE AGAINST PRIVATE JOHN CAMPBELL OF THE 26TH INDIANA VOLUNTEERS. THE TRIAL OCCURRED ABOARD A SHIP IN THE WATERS OFF THE LOUISIANA COAST.

Q: Was I drunk when I went to bed that night?

A: Do not think you were drunk at all when I saw you last. I saw you just after dark.

Q: Do you know whether I drank any after you saw me, and before I went to bed?

A: I do not.

Q: What time did I go to bed?

A: I do not know.

Q: What time did you go to bed?

A: Just after taps.

Q: Do you know of my accusing Hughes of stealing my money at any other time, or times? If so, state particularly?

A: Yes, Sir. I think I recollect you accusing him of stealing your money before. I don't recollect the time. I think it was at Rolla. I understood you to say you had a two-dollar Indiana bill which was denoted by a corner being torn off — that Hughes had given it up to you. I think I understood you to say so. I recollect another time you complained of having lost money, and you always blamed him for taking it or being concerned in taking it.

Q: Was you present when I shot Hughes?

A: No, Sir. I was not.

Q: Did you hear me say to Hughes on the morning that I shot him that if he did not find up my money, I would shoot him, or anything to that effect?

A: I think you said to Hughes that you would give him 'til breakfast-time to find up the money, and if he did not, you would shoot him, or something to that effect.

Q: What did Hughes say to this?

A: I did not hear him make any reply to anything you said to him. He laughed and turned it off.

Q: Did I say to him that morning that he had my money?

A: He said to Hughes, or close enough, that Hughes had his money or had got his money.

Q: How long was this before I shot Hughes?

A: It was from about daylight up to seven o'clock.

At this time, Private Campbell ran out of questions for the witness. The Judge Advocate and the Court also did not have any questions. Campbell then called his next defense witness to the stand and he was duly sworn to tell the truth.

Q: What is your name, age, rank, and to what command do you belong?

A: My name is Thomas Roark, age twenty-six years, am a Private in Company D, Twenty-sixth Indiana Volunteer Infantry.

Q: Do you know anything of one Moses H. Hughes stealing any money from me about May last, at Pilot Knob, Missouri?

A: I do not know of him stealing any money from you at all.

Q: Do you remember the time I shot Hughes?

A: Yes, Sir.

Q: Where did you sleep the night before?

A: I slept in the next tent to where you slept.

Q: Were you with me the evening before I shot Hughes, and if so, how late?

A: Yes, Sir. I was with you 'til dark.

Q: Do you know whether I was drunk or sober that night? When you last saw me?

A: Don't think you were very drunk.

Q: Did you hear me say anything that night about Hughes stealing any money, and if so what?

A: I did not hear you accuse any particular one of stealing your money.

Q: Did you ever hear me accuse Hughes, either to his face or when he was not present, of stealing money from me?

A: I did not.

Q: Do you know why I shot Hughes?

A: No, Sir. I do not.

Q: Did you hear me say anything when I shot Hughes, either just before, or just after shooting him?

A: No, Sir. I did not.

Q: Do you know of me getting up in the night before the shooting? If so, what happened?

A: Yes, Sir. You got up, and was making a fuss about losing your money. You said that some fellow had stolen your money — that the money was gone.

Q: What kind of tent did you have?

A: Had those little shelter tents.

Q: How many slept under one tent?

A: Two of us.

Q: Did anyone sleep with me that night?

A: Don't think there did.

Campbell then closed the testimony of this witness. The Judge Advocate and the Court did not have any questions, and the witness was dismissed. Private Campbell then called Sergeant Robinson to the stand.

Q: What is your name, age, rank, and to what command do you belong?

A: My name is Alexander Robinson, age thirty-two years, am orderly Sergeant of Company D, Twenty-sixth Indiana Volunteer Infantry.

Q: Did you examine the person of Hughes at Pilot Knob, Missouri immediately after he was shot about May last?

A: Yes, Sir, I did.

Q: What property or money, if any, did he have on his person?

A: He had twenty-six dollars in money, and a brass watch, and a pocket knife.

Q: Do you know of his having spent any money he had received since his last pay?

A: I do not know anything about his having spent any money.

Q: Do you know why I shot Hughes?

A: Well you shot him, or said you shot him because he stole your money.

Q: Do you know whether Hughes did steal my money?

A: I could not say.

Q: Was I drunk or sober when I went to bed the night before I shot Hughes?

A: I did not see you go to bed. You were both present at roll-call, and if you were any ways drunk I did not notice it.

Q: Did I want to get anybody searched the morning I shot Hughes? If so, who?

A: Yes, after Hughes was shot I believe you wanted Humphrey searched as you thought they were both concerned in the matter — this while I was taking you to the guardhouse — you blamed one pretty near as much as the other.

Q: What did I say to you that morning while you were taking me to the guardhouse?

A: When I first went to you, I asked you if you knew what you had done. You said you had done just what you said you was going to do. I asked you what you thought would be done with you. You said if you had this other man Humphreys out of the way, you should be willing to die — you expected to die anyway for what you had done.

With this great testimony on the record, Private Campbell stated he was done with the witness. The Judge Advocate and the court had no questions for the witness, and he was dismissed. The court requested Private Campbell call his next witness. Campbell stated he had no more witnesses to call. Therefore, the accused was asked if he had any statement to make to which he replied that he had and stated as follows:

"Well, Sir, twice in Springfield, Missouri, I lost my money, and when I went to Newtonia I had a two-dollar bill, marked — the corner was torn off and ink spilt on the back like a letter S turned backwards. When I went to Newtonia, I seen him have this bill and he gave it up to me. I told him it was mine and part of the eight dollars and seventy-five cents that I had lost at Springfield, Missouri. He says, handing me the bill, 'if that's yours, there it is to you.'

"At another time at Springfield, Missouri, I had seven dollars and a quarter in silver token, and he was all the one that was in the tent.

"Well, at Rolla, Missouri, or Camp Totten, he came across me and I bought two or three shirts and a silk handkerchief, and a cotton handkerchief and done them up together. I laid down and went to sleep in the tent, and he was with me. When I woke up, I had nothing left but the cotton handkerchief and two shirts, and my pocket book was also gone with nine or eleven dollars in it, and Hughes was gone also.

"On the Iron Mountain Railroad coming to St. Louis, I borrowed a dollar and a knife and it was taken from me in the night while I was asleep on the platform, and two or three days afterwards I found the knife with Hughes out at Camp Jackson. Then, I lost thirteen dollars and fifty-five cents at Pilot Knob, Missouri. I was told that he went into my tent there twice that night, and I knew he was dogging me the day before. I have hardly ever seen my pay, but I lost some of it and have even my shirts taken out of my knapsack, that is all I have to say."

Following Campbell's remarks the court adjourned. On the next day, the court resumed the case against John Campbell. The court was cleared, and after mature deliberation upon the evidence adduced, the court finds the accused John Campbell, Company D, Twenty-sixth Indiana Volunteer Infantry as follows:

Of the specification, guilty. Of the charge, guilty.

Two-thirds of the members concurring therein, and the court do therefore sentence the accused, John Campbell, Company D, Twenty-sixth Indiana Volunteer Infantry, to be shot to death with musketry at such time and place as the general commanding the department may designate, two thirds of the members concurring therein.

With the case concluded, the trial transcript went to higher military authority for review. The first endorsement was as follows,

HEADQUARTERS HERRON'S DIVISION
Carrolton, LA.
August 17, 1863.
Proceedings, findings, and sentence in this case are approved and respectfully forwarded to the General commanding the department for final action; with the recommendation that the sentence be mitigated in such manner and to such extent as the General commanding may deem proper.
F. J. HERRON,
Major General, Commanding Division.

Second Endorsement
HEADQUARTERS DEPARTMENT OF THE GULF
New Orleans, LA
September 10, 1863
The proceedings, findings, and sentence in the case of Private John Campbell, Co. 'D' 26th Indiana Volunteers are approved, but on the recommendation of the officer convening the court, the sentence is suspended until the pleasure of the President can be known. It is however the opinion of the Major General Commanding that justice as well as a proper regard for the discipline of this Army, require the execution of this sentence.
NATHANIEL BANKS,
Major General.

The trial transcript was then sent to the Judge Advocate General of the United States, Joseph Holt. Holt reviewed the case and presented a written summation of the case as follows.

October, 19, 1863, Private Campbell of the 26th Indiana was charged with murder in that on the 28th of May, 1863, he willfully, feloniously, and with malice aforethought killed one Hughes, an enlisted man of the same regiment. The proof is clear that it was an atrocious murder, committed in cold blood and with premeditation. The accused simply claims in his statement of defense that the man whom he killed had repeatedly stolen money from him.

General Herron, who ordered the court, recommends some mitigation of the sentence, and General Banks therefore suspends its execution, and submits the case for the action of the President. At the same time expressing the opinion that justice, as well as the discipline of his Army, requires the sentence to be enforced. The opinion of General Banks is fully concurred in.

J. HOLT,
Judge Advocate General.

President Lincoln's action was swift and brief. Lincoln wrote:

Sentence approved.
A. Lincoln

Judge Advocate General's Office.
October 19th 1863.

Private Campbell of the 26th Ind. was charged with murder. In that on the 28th of May 63. he wilfully, feloniously, and with malice aforethought killed one Hughes an enlisted man of the same regiment.

The proof is clear that it was an atrocious murder committed in cold blood, and with premeditation.

The accused simply claims in his statement of defence, that the man whom he killed had repeatedly stolen money from him.

Genl. Herron who ordered the court recommends some mitigation of the sentence, and Genl. Banks therefore suspends its execution and submits the case for the action of the President: at the same time expressing the opinion that justice as well as the discipline of his army requires the sentence to be enforced.

The opinion of General Banks is fully concurred in.

Holt

Judge Advocate General

Sentence approved

A. Lincoln

PRESIDENT LINCOLN APPROVED THE DEATH SENTENCE OF PRIVATE JOHN CAMPBELL FOR THE COLD-BLOODED MURDER OF PRIVATE MOSES H. HUGHES, WHO WAS SHOT IN THE HEAD WHILE EATING HIS BREAKFAST.

In this case, the trial took place on board the ship *Tecumseh*, off Port Hudson, Louisiana. The American Civil War generated a huge amount of naval sea actions off the coasts of our nation, and around the world. As a point of interest, the *USS Tecumseh* was involved in a fight on August 6, 1864, in the waters off Mobile Bay, Alabama. The ship was blown up, and sank in a matter of minutes. The Union Naval crew lost close to one hundred men. Only two officers and thirteen seamen were saved. There was a great argument at the time as to whether the ship was sunk by cannon fire from Confederate Fort Morgan, or by a torpedo. The torpedo of that era was a naval mine. The Confederates would anchor the mines across a point to be defended, or float them on the current into Union ships. One Confederate report at the time said the ship "hit a torpedo, and sank in thirty seconds." The *USS Tecumseh* that was sunk was referred to as a monitor ship. The Campbell trial reportedly took place on the steamer *Tecumseh.* I can find only one record of a ship named *Tecumseh* in the *Official Record of The Rebellion* series. I believe they are the same ship, but I'm not positive.

As stated above, naval action occurred around the world. Probably the most famous sea battle was the fight between the *USS Kearsarge*, and the Confederate States Ship (CSS) *Alabama*. The *CSS Alabama* had been roaming the sea for about two years as a commerce raider. The *Alabama* had sunk or captured some sixty-five federal ships. On June 19, 1864, the *USS Kearsarge* located the *CSS Alabama*, and sunk her in a sea battle just outside the port of Cherbourg, France.

The *CSS Shenandoah* operated as a commerce raider and roamed over large sections of the ocean looking for ships bringing supplies to Union ports. There were quite a few Union naval vessels assigned to chase after her, but they never got her. At the war's end, the *Shenandoah* put into a British port and surrendered to the British.

Chapter 6

The Free Press

During the Civil War, a disloyal act could land a person in a very large tub of hot water. One way to get such a bath was to be critical of the war effort, the Union Army, or the President. At the start of the war, many government officials took these disloyal acts quite seriously. As the war progressed, some things began to change and it became more acceptable to register complaints about the people in charge of the war effort. In this chapter, a newspaper editor takes a few swipes at the President and is hammered down for his effort. Later on in the war, it became more acceptable to take critical note of the actions of the President. The Presidents' wife, Mary Todd Lincoln, became the subject of many rumors and some published reports that were quite vicious in nature.

Mrs. Lincoln had grown up in Lexington, Kentucky. She was regarded by the Washington D.C. social and political crowd as a southern supporter. The nice rumors named her as a steadfast, loyal, Confederate Belle. The nasty rumors labeled her as a rebel spy. Mary Lincoln had four brothers in Confederate uniform. Her full brother was a doctor in the Confederate Army. Her three half-brothers also wore gray, and all three died for the south. In addition, three of her brothers-in-law wore gray. Little wonder she was viewed as pro-Southern. Everyone seemed to forget that Kentucky was also a border state and had divided loyalties throughout its population. During the war, Mary Lincoln was trapped in her position as the wife of the President who was defending the Union.

The charge of aid to the enemy was easy to acquire, but hard to defend. As you read the details of this trial, try to imagine if something along these lines were brought forward as a charge against some modern-day newspaper like The New York Times. There would be one very large political and legal uprising, and it would continue for many years. But here in the Civil War, the fate of the nation was at stake, and the battle for the heart and minds of the American people was but part of the war — so public newspaper reporting was closely watched. As you read the details remember that so often when faced with a major crisis, political and military leaders tend to try and crush hard-won freedoms in the rush to cure the new problem.

COLUMBIA, Mo., Tuesday, February 25, 1862.

The commission proceeded to the trial of Edmund J. Ellis, a citizen of Boone County, Missouri, who being called into court had the above order read in his hearing and was asked if he objected to be tried by any member named in detail, to which he replied in the negative.

The commission was then duly sworn in the presence of the accused, and the Judge Advocate duly sworn by the president, also in the presence of the accused.

The prisoner was then arraigned on the following charges and specifications:

Charge 1: The publication of information for the benefit of the enemy and encouraging resistance to the Government and laws of the United States.

Specification 1: In this, that in a public newspaper published in the town of Columbia, county of Boone, State of Missouri, called The Boone County Standard of which paper the said Edmund J. Ellis was editor and proprietor on the fifteenth day of November, A.D. 1861, the said Edmund J. Ellis permitted and caused to be printed and published an article, entitled "Letters from Our Army," design and object of which publication was to encourage and further rebellion against the existing Government of the United States.

Specification 2: Printed and published and caused to be printed and published an article entitled "To the Civil Officers of Boone County," which said article contained treasonable matter and was designed and intended to encourage resistance to the Government and laws of the United States.

Specification 3: Printed and published and caused to be printed and published a certain article entitled "Root, Abe, or Die," which said article was designed and intended to encourage resistance to the Government and laws of the United States.

Specification 4: Printed and published and caused to be printed and published a certain article entitled "The U.S. Flag — Rebellion," which said article contained treasonable matter and was designed and intended to encourage resistance to the Government and laws of the United States.

Specification 5: Printed and published and caused to be printed and published a certain article entitled "Carrier's Address," which said article contained treasonable matter and was designed and intended to encourage resistance to the Government and laws of the United States.

Specification 6: Printed and published and caused to be printed and published a certain article entitled "News from General Price," the design and object of which article was to give information to the enemies of the Government and to encourage resistance to the Government and laws of the United States.

Charge 2: Violation of the laws of war by the publication within the lines of the troops of the United States in a public newspaper of articles and information intended and designed to comfort the enemy and incite persons to rebellion against the Government of the United States.

Specification 1: In this, that in a public newspaper printed and published in the town of Columbia, county of Boone, State of Missouri, styled and called The Boone County Standard of which said newspaper the said Edmund J. Ellis was the editor and proprietor, the said Edmund J. Ellis on the twenty-ninth day of November, 1861, at Columbia did publish and cause to be published a certain treasonable and seditious commu-

nication, via, a letter addressed to the people of Kentucky and signed by J. C. Breckinridge, by which publication the said Edmund J. Ellis designed and intended to comfort the enemy and incite to rebellion against the Government of the United States persons within the lines of the troops of the United States.

Specification 2: In this, that the said Edmund J. Ellis did print and publish and cause to be printed and published and circulated within the lines of the United States a certain pamphlet styled "To the Patriot Army of Missouri," which pamphlet was calculated and designed to give aid to the enemy and to encourage and incite to acts of insurrection the people living within these said lines of troops; which pamphlet is hereto appended and marked. All this at or near Columbia, Missouri, on or about the first day of October 1861.

Specification 3: That in a public newspaper printed and published in the town of Columbia, Boone County, Missouri, known and styled as The Boone County Standard of which said newspaper the said Edmund J. Ellis was the editor and proprietor, the said Edmund J. Ellis did on the sixth day of December, 1861, at Columbia publish and cause to be published certain articles, via, a treasonable and seditious article styled "Proclamation to the people of Central and North Missouri" and signed "Sterling Price, Major General Commanding," and a certain other treasonable and seditious article entitled "Convention between the State of Missouri and the Government of the Confederate States," and signed "E. C. Cabell, Thomas L. Snead and R. M. T. Hunter," also a certain other treasonable and seditious article entitled "Message of President Jefferson Davis to the Congress of the Confederate States" and signed "Jefferson Davis, Richmond, November 18, 1861. "All of which articles were published with the intent and design of giving comfort to the enemy and of inciting to rebellion against the Government of the United States persons within the lines of the troops of the United States.

To which several charges and specifications the accused interposed his plea to the jurisdiction of the court as follows, to wit:

The accused, Edmund J. Ellis, objects and excepts to the jurisdiction of the court or military commission on all the matters and things stated in the two charges and the various specifications hereunder on the grounds following, to wit: That the matters and things therein stated and charged (admitting them to be true, the truth of which, however, he controverts) are wholly and exclusively of civil cognizance.

Second. Because there is no supervision of the arm of civil power, no obstruction to judicial process and hence no sudden and extraordinary necessity (so far as the present case is concerned) for the intervention of a summary military commission or any military authority whatever.

Third. Because the matters and things stated in the said charges and specifications if criminal at all are violations of the Constitution and civil law of the land for the punishment of which tribunals of justice are provided, military commissions being unknown to the Constitution and laws of the United States.

Whereupon the court having been cleared proceeded to consider said plea and after mature deliberation overruled the said plea.

Whereupon the court having been again opened and the decision announced to the prisoner the prisoner pleaded as follows, to wit:

To the specifications, not guilty, and to the charges, not guilty.

The court then adjourned at six p.m. until ten o'clock Wednesday morning, February 26, 1862.

LEWIS MERRILL,

Colonel Regiment Merrill's Horse, President Military Commission.

ROBERT A. HOWARD,

First Lieutenant, Merrill's Horse, Recorder Military Commission.

WEDNESDAY, February 26, 1862.

The court met pursuant to adjournment, all the members present.

Edward Reynolds, a witness for the prosecution, being duly sworn testified as follows:

By the Judge Advocate:

Q: What is your age, place of residence and occupation?

A: I am nineteen years old; reside in Columbia; I am a printer by trade.

Q: Are you acquainted with the accused, Edmund J. Ellis? If yes, state how long you have known the said Ellis and what is his occupation or business.

A: I know the accused. Have known him about ten months. He (Ellis) is a printer by trade and has been ever since I have known him the editor of The Boone County Standard.

(Here the witness was handed copies of the newspaper styled The Boone County Standard for the following dates, respectively, to wit: Friday, November 15, 1861; Friday, November 22, 1861; Friday, November 29, 1861; Friday, December 6, 1861; Friday, December 13, 1861; Friday, January 3, 1862; Friday, February 7, 1862.)

Q: Examine the papers shown to you and state whether or not they are copies of the paper you have just referred to, and whatever you know with regard to their publication with your means of knowledge.

A: These are copies of The Boone County Standard that I have worked upon for the last nine months. Mr. Ellis, the accused, was the only editor I ever knew for the paper.

(The papers thus referred to were then offered in evidence and no objection being made accepted, and are hereto attached, marked respectively exhibits B, C, D, E, F, G and H and made part of the testimony for the prosecution in this case.)

Q: Examine the articles styled "Letter from our Army" and "To the Civil Officers of Boone County" in the paper now shown you and state what if anything you know of their authorship.

(Here the witness was handed newspaper marked Exhibit B.)

A: Both articles are communications. I do not know who wrote them. The first I know to be communication; the other I believe to be.

Q: Examine the paper now shown to you and state what if anything you know of the authorship of the article entitled "The U.S. Flag — Rebellion."

(Here the witness was handed newspaper marked Exhibit F.)

A: I do not recollect the author of that if I know him. I suppose it to be editorial.

Q: Examine the paper now shown to you and state what if anything you know of the authorship of the article entitled "Carrier's Address."

(Here the witness was handed newspaper marked Exhibit G.)

A: I believe the man's name who wrote it was Dysen.

Q: Examine the pamphlet now shown to you and state what if anything you know of its publication; where it was printed, by whom, how many copies were printed, by whom circulated, by whom written. State all you know connected with it.

(Here the witness was handed pamphlet "To the Patriot Army of Missouri.")

A: It was printed in The Boone County Standard office. I think three hundred copies were printed. Don't know who wrote it. Don't know who circulated it. Don't know who it was printed for.

The pamphlet was here offered in evidence and no objection having been made accepted, and is hereto attached, marked Exhibit A and made part of the testimony for the prosecution in this case.

By a member:

Q: What became of the copies of the pamphlet marked A of which you say some three hundred copies were printed

A: They were taken from the office. Don't know who by or where.

The prosecution here rested and the prisoner produced the following evidence:

Edward Reynolds, a witness for the defense having been duly sworn testified as follows:

By the Prisoner:

Q: Do you know of any copies of said pamphlet having been circulated by Edmund J. Ellis, or by anyone else at his instance?

A: I do not.

Q: Was your position as an employee such that you had a good opportunity of knowing whether it was so circulated?

A: Yes.

At this time the defense rested its case and the prisoner, Edmund J. Ellis, decided not to make any statement to the court. Ellis then submitted the case to the court. The court was then cleared and the members deliberated their verdict.

The members of the commission returned with a verdict of "guilty" on all charges and specifications.

And the commission does therefore sentence him, the said Edmund J. Ellis, to be placed and kept outside the lines of the State of Missouri during the war and that the press, types, furniture and material of the printing office of The Boone County Standard be confiscated and sold for the use of the United States.

LEWIS MERRILL,

Colonel Regiment Merrill's Horse, President Military Commission.

ROBERT A. HOWARD,

First Lieutenant, Merrill's Horse, Recorder Military Commission.

Finding and sentence approved. The press, types, furniture and material of the printing office of The Boone County Standard will remain in charge of the quartermaster's department 'til further orders. The proper commanding officer will see that the prisoner, Edmund J. Ellis, is placed outside of the State of Missouri. Should he return within the lines of this State during the war without proper permission he will be arrested and placed in close confinement in the Alton military prison.

H. W. HALLECK,
Major General.

Chapter 7

The Horse Thief

As the war continued, more men were enlisted into the U.S. Army to fight the rebels. A growing pool of manpower also led to more court-martial cases for the Union Army. Some of the new men could seem to find many ways to commit a crime. In this chapter, a young lad was suspected of violating the trust placed in him by becoming a common thief.

The Sherman Dodge case began on August 19, 1863, at Rolla, Missouri. A general court-martial board was appointed by special order no. 129. On August 21, 1863, the board was in session with five officers to serve as board members: Major W. H. Dale of the Second Wisconsin Cavalry Volunteers was named as the Judge Advocate to prosecute the case against Private Sherman Dodge.

> *The court proceeded to the trial of Sherman Dodge, Private of Company A, Second Wisconsin Cavalry Volunteers, who was brought before the court and having heard the order convening the board read, was asked if he had any objection to any member named in the order, to which he replied that he did not.*
>
> *The court was then duly sworn by the Judge Advocate, and the Judge Advocate was duly sworn by the President of the court, all in the presence of the accused. The Judge Advocate here asked the accused if he desired to introduce counsel, and he replied he did not.*
>
> *The Judge Advocate then requested all persons subpoenaed as witnesses to withdraw from the tent, and wait until called for. The accused, Sherman Dodge, Private Company*

A, Second Wisconsin Cavalry was then arraigned on the following charges and specifications:

Charge, Larceny of Government Property.

Specification: In this, that he, Sherman Dodge, Private of Company A of the Second Regiment of Wisconsin Cavalry Volunteers, on the nineteenth day of May A.D. 1863, at Lake Spring, Dent County, in the state of Missouri, did feloniously steal, and take away, one horse of the value of fifty-five dollars, the property of the United States, and these being in the possession of the Commanding Officer of the company, and did there and then unlawfully sell the horse, appropriating the proceeds of said sale to his own use.

Private Dodge pleaded not guilty, and the trial began. The first witness was called to the witness chair and duly sworn to tell the truth.

Q: What is your name and rank and to what command do you belong?

A: My name is Dwight G. Beagle, am Corporal of Company A, Second Wisconsin Cavalry.

Q: Do you know the accused, Sherman Dodge?

A: Yes, Sir. He belongs to the same company that I do.

Q: Do you know anything of a horse being taken from your company in May, last? If so, describe the horse.

A: I know there was one missing. It was a gray mare, she was usually rode by John Hawley, bugler.

Q: State under what circumstances the horse disappeared.

A: The horse was among the company horses at night, and in the morning, she was gone.

Q: Was there anyone on stable guard that night? If so, who were they?

A: There was a stable guard, but I don't know who they were.

Q: When and where was this horse lost?

A: It was at Lake Spring, Missouri. I should think it was about the twentieth day of May, 1863. I am not positive on the date.

Q: Have you since that horse was missing, heard the accused say anything in reference to the horse? If so, state what he said.

A: I heard him say that he knew where she was. He said she was in the First Iowa Cavalry. I think he said he took her to the First Iowa Cavalry. I am not quite certain that he said that. He said he did not get anything for the horse.

Q: When and where did you hear the accused make those statements, and who was present?

A: It was sometime about the middle of June, last. It was at camp near Rolla. Sergeant Palmer, Lieutenant Wilkins, the accused, and myself were present.

The witness was dismissed and the second prosecution witness was called to the witness chair and duly sworn to tell the truth.

Q: What is your name, rank, and to what command do you belong?

A: My name is George F. Wilkins, am Second Lieutenant of Company A, Second Wisconsin Cavalry Volunteers.

Q: Do you know the accused, Sherman Dodge?

A: I do, Sir. He belongs to the same company with me.

Q: Do you know anything of a horse being taken from the company sometime in May, last? If so, describe the horse.

A: The horse was a gray mare. She was usually rode by Bugler John Hawley. The mare was missing on the morning of the nineteenth of May, 1863. The accused, Sherman Dodge was on stable guard that night. I mean the night of the eighteenth. We could not get any clue to the horse at the time. About the middle of June, I went to the tent in which the accused stayed to inquire for some revolvers that had been taken from that and another tent, that day. He said he knew nothing about them. I asked him about the mare, he said he took the mare to the First Iowa Cavalry and sold her to one of that regiment, but he received no money for her.

114

usually rode by John Hawley Bugler

Ques J.ad — State under what Circumstances the horse disappeared,

Ans — The horse, was then among the Company horses at night, and in the Morning, she was gone.

Ques J.ad — Was there any One on Stable guard that night, if so, who were they,

Ans — There was a Stable guard but I dont Know who they were.

Ques J ad — When and where was the horse lost.

Ans, — It was at Lake Spring Mo. I should think, it was about the 30th day of May 1863, I am not positive as to the date,

Ques J a. — Have you since that horse was Missing, heard the accused say anything, in reference to the horse, if so State what he said,

Ans — I heard him say, that he knew

A SAMPLE PAGE FROM THE LARCENY TRIAL OF PRIVATE SHERMAN DODGE, WHO WAS CHARGED WITH ABSCONDING WITH A UNION ARMY'S OLD GRAY MARE AT LAKE SPRING IN DENT COUNTY, MISSOURI.

Q: Did he say anything as to the time, when he took her there?

A: I believe not, Sir.

Q: State to whom the horse belonged.

A: It was a government horse used in the company as public property.

Q: What was the horse worth?

A: I think at the time the horse was taken she was worth from fifty to fifty-five dollars. She had the grease heel [Author's note: grease heel is a fungus type infection of the horse hoof] and we intended to turn her over to the quartermaster as unserviceable.

Q: Who were present at the time you heard the accused make the statement, to which you have testified?

A: Corporal Beagle and Sergeant Palmer were present.

Q: Have you ever found the horse?

A: We have not.

Q: Did you have him state anything in reference to any bargain made with the person to whom he sold the horse?

A: No, Sir.

Question by the Court: Where was the First Iowa at that time?

A: At the time she was taken, they were encamped about a half-mile from our camp. At the time the accused made those statements, I think the First Iowa Cavalry had gone towards Pilot Knob.

Lieutenant Wilkins was dismissed and the next witness called and sworn.

Q: What is your name, rank, and to what command do you belong?

A: My name is Andrew J. Palmer, am First Sergeant of Company A, Second Wisconsin Cavalry.

Q: Do you know the accused, Sherman Dodge?

A: I do, he belongs to the same company as me.

Q: Do you know anything of a horse being taken from the company sometime in May, last? If so, describe the horse.

A: There were three horses taken in May, last. One we recovered, the other two we did not. Two were taken on the night of the seventeenth of May, and one on the night of the eighteenth or nineteenth.

Q: Describe the last one taken.

A: It was a light gray mare, usually rode by Bugler, John Hawley.

Q: State, if you know, any of the circumstances under which she was taken.

A: She was missing in the morning of the nineteenth. She was there the night before. There were two men sent out to look for her, but they did not find her.

Q: Have you, since the mare was missing, heard the accused say anything in reference to the mare, and what became of her?

A: I have. I asked the accused on the twenty-third of June, last, if he knew where that mare was and he said he did. Lieutenant Wilkins and Corporal Beagle were present, at all times. Lieutenant Wilkins then asked him where she was. The accused answered, 'I suppose she is in the First Iowa Cavalry.' Lieutenant Wilkins asked how she came there. I think I asked him if he received any money for her, and he said he did not.

Q: What was the value of that mare?

A: She was worth about forty or fifty dollars.

Q: Where was the First Iowa Cavalry at the time the accused made those statements?

A: I don't know. They had left some time before that for Pilot Knob.

Q: Where was the accused on the night the mare was missing?

A: He was on stable guard on the third relief. The night was divided with three reliefs, and his relief would commence about two o'clock in the morning.

The prosecution here closed.

Andrew Lowry a witness for the defense being first duly sworn testified as follows:

Questions by the prisoner:

Q: What is your name and to what command do you belong?

A: My name is Andrew Lowry, am a private of Company A, Second Wisconsin Cavalry.

Q: Do you know the accused, Sherman Dodge?

A: Yes, Sir. He belongs to the same company with me.

Q: Do you know anything of a horse, known as the John Hawley mare, being missed from the company sometime in May?

A: Yes, Sir. I remember the circumstances.

Q: Where were you on the night the mare was lost?

A: I was in camp. I was on stable guard.

Q: What relief was yours that night?

A: Mine was the first relief.

Q: Who stood the second?

A: Peter Milroy.

Q: Do you know, if the mare was there when you was relieved?

A: No, Sir. When I went on guard I took that mare from the picket rope, and tied her to a stake where my horse was tied, and fed her, and when I was relieved, she was not there.

Q: Did you see anyone around there during your relief?

A: No, Sir. Except a couple of burr boys who were on guard. Sherman Dodge was there with me most of the time. We had a fire, and he was by the fire. He was sitting up and was not asleep. He was there when I was relieved.

Q: At what time did your relief commence, and at what time were you relieved?

A: I went on at eight o'clock, and was relieved about half past eleven.

Questions by Judge Advocate on cross-examination:

Q: Had Dodge been to bed during that time?

A: No, Sir. I believe not.

Q: Did you have any conversation with him about that mare during the night?

A: No, Sir.

Q: Have you since that heard him say anything about what became of that mare?

A: No, Sir.

The accused having no further evidence to offer submitted the case without remarks. The Judge Advocate doing the same.

The court was then cleared for deliberation, and having maturely considered the evidence adduced, do find the accused Sherman Dodge, Private of Company A, Second Wisconsin Cavalry;

Of the specification to the charge, guilty.

Of the charge, guilty.

And the court do therefore sentence him, Sherman Dodge, Private of Company A, Second Wisconsin Cavalry, to be confined, at hard labor, in the penitentiary of the State of Missouri, for the term of six months and stoppage of pay and allowances for the term of three months.

The next entry in the transcript was an extremely brief note by the higher reviewing authority. The note read:

Finding and sentence approved,
Wm. A. DAVIS,
Brigadier General, Command.

Private Dodge of the Second Wisconsin Cavalry was charged with larceny of government property. Specification in this, that on the 19th day of May, 1863 he feloniously stole and took away a horse of the value of fifty-five dollars the property of the United States, then in the possession of the commanding officer and unlawfully sold the horse appropriating the proceeds to his own use. The proof is that the horse was missed from the stable of the camp on the morning of the 20th of May, and though search was made, could not be found. About a month afterwards, the accused admitted to an officer of the regiment that he sold her to someone in the First Iowa Cavalry (which, at the time the horse was taken, encamped nearby) but stated that he had not received any pay.

The horse, it appears, was not of much value, and it had been determined to turn it over to the Quartermaster as unserviceable, and a sale of the horse to any person in another cavalry regiment would seem improbable. The prisoner could have no motive for admitting the theft and sale, for the admission was made a month subsequent to the loss of the animal and he was under no constraint at the time.

The court in view of the statements of the accused in connection with the proof that he was on guard at the stable on the night the horse was lost, found him guilty as charged and sentenced him to be confined in the Missouri Penitentiary for the term of six months and to stoppage of all pay and allowance for three months. General Schofield not being empowered to enforce the confinement forwards the record for the orders of the President.

J. HOLT,
Judge Advocate General.

The reply of President Lincoln in this case was very brief:

Sentence Approved.
A. Lincoln,
February 9, 1864.

powered to enforce the confinement, forwards the record for the orders of the President.

J. Holt —

Judge Advocate General.

Sentence approved

A. Lincoln

Feb. 9. 1864,

THE CASE OF A MINOR HORSE THIEF RATED THE ATTENTION OF THE PRESIDENT OF THE UNITED STATES. PRESIDENT ABRAHAM LINCOLN REVIEWED AND APPROVED A SIX-MONTH PRISON TERM FOR PRIVATE SHERMAN DODGE.

Chapter 8

The Goose Case

Since the dawn of recorded history soldiers have always complained about the quality and quantity of the military food they have been ordered to consume. The search for good food has been the cause of a lot of grief for many an army. In this case, a young Union soldier on a long road march had a chance encounter with a farmer who had a fat goose. But, was the goose worth the price each man had to pay?

The charge was Murder. The specification stated:

In this, that he, Jasper Laster, Private of Company H., Third Regiment of Cavalry, Missouri State Militia, did on the twenty-third day of December 1863, on the road from Farmington, Missouri, to Pilot Knob, Missouri, kill by shooting one Michael Larabe, a citizen of St. Francis County, Missouri.

The court asked for a formal plea from Pvt. Laster and his plea was guilty. But like so many other defendants, he felt his case was not that simple. Yes, he had shot the farmer, but there were good reasons for his actions. And so, he wished to present witnesses' testimony. The court agreed to listen to the testimony, and Pvt. Laster called his first witness to the stand and the actual trial began.

Private John Lynch of Company H., Third Missouri Cavalry Missouri State Militia, a witness for the defense being duly sworn states that on or about the twenty-third day of December 1863, Laster, the accused, spoke to Michael Larabe and asked him how he was — he said it was none of his business — he wanted to buy a goose from Larabe and offered him two bits for it — and he would not take less than fifty cents — If you lay a hand on that goose I will shoot you. Laster answered "You will, eh!!" Then, Larabe said, "If you are a better soldier than I am, let's shoot," and handed out with his pistol or revolver.

Question by the Court: Did you see Jasper Laster shoot Michael Larabe?

A: Yes. As I was moving off, I called to them not to shoot.

Question by the Court: Do you know if the accused and the deceased was acquainted before the shooting?

A: I do not know.

Question by the Court: Did the accused address the deceased by name when they met in the road?

A: No, Sir. Not that I know of.

Question by the Court: By what authority was you and Laster on the road?

A: By the order of the Captain, I suppose.

Question by the Court: For what purpose was you and Laster traveling together?

A: For no purpose in the world, but to come to Pilot Knob that I know of.

Question by the Court: Did Michael Larabe advance towards Laster with his pistol drawn, or did he stand by his property?

A: He advanced.

Question by Judge Advocate: Was Michael Larabe on his wagon when he was shot?

A: No, Sir.

Question by the Court: How far was he from the wagon?

A: I could not tell, but I think a few steps.

Question by the Court: Was he before the wagon or behind it?

A: He was kind of off to one side.

Question by the Court: On which side?

A: On the near side, as he was driving.

Question by the Court: What kind of team was it?

Question
Did you not the accused threaten or say that he would take the [illegible]
Ans
he told Leiber that two bits was enough for the goods
Question by the Court.
Did the accused get the goods in possession during the [illegible].
Ans
No, sir — the goods remained on the waggon the best of my opinion
Question by the Court.
Was not the accused drinking that day.
Ans
To the best of my opinion he was drinking that day — we was all drinking that morning
Question by the Court.

A SAMPLE PAGE FROM THE TRIAL OF PRIVATE JASPER LASTER.

A: I do not know, but I think it was an Ox team.

Question by the Court: Was the team moving at the time of the shooting?

A: I do not know.

Question by the Court: How long was it from your coming up with the team until the shooting took place?

A: About five minutes; they talked mighty quick.

Question by the Court: Had you passed the wagon before the shooting took place?

A: I think we had.

Question by the Court: Had Laster turned back to shoot?

A: To the best of my opinion, Laster did not advance from where he met Larabe, the deceased.

Question by the Court: Did you meet Larabe in the road, or overtake him on the way?

A: I never took notice of which way the team was going.

Question by the Court: Did Larabe, the deceased, give the accused any occasion to shoot in self-preservation?

A: He drew his pistol first.

Question by the Court: Did not the accused Laster threaten to take the goose at all hazards?

A: No, Sir.

Question by the Court: What was the cause of conflict between the accused and the deceased?

A: The price of the goose.

Question by the Court: Did the accused threaten or say he would take the goose anyhow?

A: He told Larabe that two bits was enough for the goose.

Question by the Court: Did the accused get the goose in his possession during the quarrel?

A: No, Sir. The goose remained on the wagon the best of my opinion.

Question by the Court: Was not the accused drinking that day?

A: To the best of my opinion, he was drinking that day. We was all drinking that morning.

Question by the Court: By whose orders was you all drinking?

A: I do not know of any orders.

Question by the Court: Was not the accused straggling from his command when he did the shooting?

A: No, Sir.

Question by the Court: How far was he from his command at the time?

A: About a mile or half, a mile maybe.

Question by the Court: Had he orders to remain so far behind as a rear guard?

A: I do not know that he did.

Question by the Court: By whose orders was you behind the column?

A: By no orders.

Question by the Court: Did you start with the column from Farmington?

A: No, Sir.

Question by the Court: Did the accused start with the command from Farmington?

A: To the best of my opinion, he did fine; I was behind when they started.

Question by the Court: How far did you travel with the accused before the shooting?

A: I could not tell.

Question by the Court: How far from Farmington did you overtake the accused?

A: I did not notice; he was with the rest when I overtook him.

At this time the court adjourned until ten o'clock a.m. on Wednesday the sixth day of January 1864.

Wednesday, January 6th, 1864, the court resumed pursuant to adjournment. Present the same members as yesterday; the accused was also present and the Judge Advocate. The preceding hearing being read over to the court by the Judge Advocate.

Private William Wilkerson of Company H, Third Regiment, Missouri State Militia, a witness for the defense being duly sworn states that he is acquainted with Jasper Laster the accused.

Question by Accused: State to all here what you know in relation to the shooting of Michael Larabe, a citizen of St. Francis County Missouri, on the road from Farmington,

Missouri, to Pilot Knob, Missouri, on the twenty-third day of December 1863.

A: I do not know anything about the shooting — but saw him after he was shot. I went back when I heard the man was shot — and helped carry him to a house on the Pilot Knob Road.

Question by Accused: What did the deceased say?

A: He said that if this man had not shot him, then he would have shot him.

Question by the Court: Had the deceased any arms about him when you came up to him?

A: He had a pistol.

Question by the Court: In what position was the pistol?

A: It was belted around him.

Question by the Court: Was the pistol loaded?

A: I never noticed — whether it was or not.

Question by the Court: Was the pistol in the holster?

A: It was.

Question by the Court: Do you think the deceased could have returned his pistol to the holster himself after being shot?

A: I do not know what he could have done.

Question by the Court: Was the prisoner drunk on the day of the shooting?

A: I do not know; he appeared as usual.

The prisoner having no further testimony to offer, the court was closed and proceeded to deliberate on the testimony adduced.

The court after mature deliberation on the testimony adduced find the prisoner, Private Jasper Laster of Company H, Third Regiment of Cavalry, Missouri State Militia as follows, to wit:

Of the specification, guilty.

Of the charge, guilty.

And do therefore sentence him, Private Jasper Laster of Company H, Third Cavalry, M. S. M., to be shot to death by musketry at such time and place as the General Commanding may direct. Two thirds of the members concurring.

Capt. JAMES W. McFADEN,
Third Cavalry Missouri State Militia, President.
1st Lt. THOMAS H. MACKLIND,
Third Cavalry Missouri State Militia, Judge Advocate.

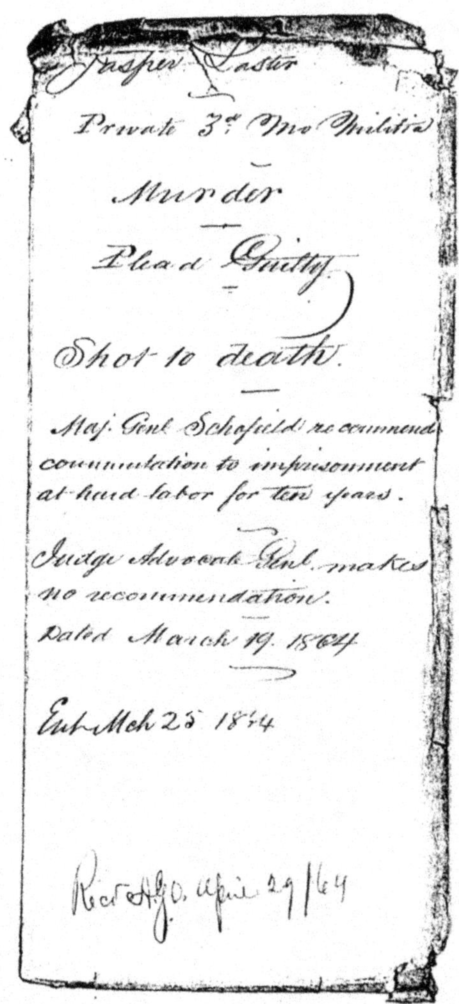

Jasper Laster

Private 3rd Mo Militia

Murder

Plead Guilty

Shot to death.

Maj. Genl Schofield recommend commutation to imprisonment at hard labor for ten years.

Judge Advocate Genl. makes no recommendation.

Dated March 19. 1864

Ent Mch 25 1864

Recd A.G.O. April 29/64

THE COVER RECORD FROM THE FILE ON THE TRIAL OF PRIVATE JASPER LASTER WHO WAS CHARGED WITH MURDER OVER THE POSSESSION OF A GOOSE.

The next entry in the case file was a memo that sent the trial record from the Judge Advocate's office in St. Louis, Missouri, to Washington, D.C. The wording on the memo was as follows:

Transmitted herewith for the action of the President are the proceedings of Private Jasper Laster 3rd Cav. M. S. M. and Henry Sytchliter of Co. G, 2nd Cav. M. S. M., both sentenced "to be shot to death," and attention is respectfully called to the recommendation endorsed thereon.

Along with the memo from the Judge Advocate's office, went the recommendation of Union General, John Schofield.

General Schofield wrote:

Finding and sentence confirmed. Proceedings respectfully forwarded for the action of the President with the recommendation that the punishment be commuted to imprisonment at hard labor for 10 years. The execution of the sentence is suspended until the pleasure of the President herein can be known.

On March 19th 1864, Joseph Holt, the Judge Advocate General of the United States, reviewed the case. J. A. Holt's written summation of the case was as follows:

Private Jasper Laster of the 3rd Missouri Militia Volunteers was convicted of murder and sentenced to be shot.

General Schofield suspends the execution of the sentence and submits the case for the action of the President, recommending commutation to imprisonment at hard labor for ten years. The prisoner plead guilty to the charge and specification wherein the shooting of a citizen named Larabe, while on the march from Farmington, Missouri, to Pilot Knob, Missouri, on the 23rd day of December A.D. 1863 was alleged.

No testimony was offered by the prosecution. The prisoner called as a witness an enlisted man who swore that Laster met or overtook Larabe on the road and asked him to sell him a goose, offering 'two bits' for it. Larabe declined to sell it for less than fifty cents. After some dispute, the witness says that Larabe drew a pistol whereupon Laster fired and killed him.

Another enlisted man called as a witness for the defense testified that he heard that a man had been shot, and upon going to the place where the killing occurred found the dead man with his pistol in his holster, belted around his body.

From this it would appear that no attempt was made by the deceased to shoot Laster, and the crime was doubtless a willful, unprovoked murder.

Once again, the last stop was the desk of Abraham Lincoln. In April of 1864, he placed the last entry into the file:

Sentence commuted to confinement at hard labor in the penitentiary for ten years.

A. Lincoln

death by musketry at such time and place as the Comdg Genl may direct

Sentence commuted to confinement, at hard labor in the Penitentiary, for ten years.

A. Lincoln

April 21, 1864

Chapter 9

Muse Kirby

In this chapter, an eighteen-year-old youth from the Missouri Boot Heel runs head-on into the brick wall known as the Civil War. He must pay a terrible price for his discovery of how deadly things can turn during a time of war. As you follow his story, one can only try to understand the thoughts and actions he must have experienced. The actions of a man like Muse Kirby would be hard for us to understand today. We have all forgotten that the Civil War featured some 3.5 million men in uniform. Each of these men had a story to tell of wartime experience. This pool of war experience remains a part of our national history. It would be impossible to ever account for all of the events that occurred in the war. Remember, more than six hundred thousand of these stories ended in death. Another four hundred-ten thousand men were made prisoners of war and suffered under terrible conditions in prison camps. Many others received battle wounds that troubled them for the rest of their lives. Most of us don't realize just how vast an enterprise the Civil War was during the four years of the war.

The following Union Army General Orders No. 249 lists Muse Kirby as but one of three men who were tried and convicted by a Union Army Military Tribunal. All three men were sentenced to death after their trial. All three men had their case referred to President Lincoln for final review. We will learn all about Muse Kirby in this chapter, but the full story on the other two men will remain a mystery. Maybe at some future time we can look into their story and present their cases to the world.

GENERAL COURT MARTIAL, } WAR DEPARTMENT,
ADJUTANT GENERAL'S OFFICE,
ORDERS No. 249. } *Washington, August* 18, 1864.

I...Before a Military Commission, which convened at Saint Louis, Missouri, August 19, 1863, pursuant to Special Orders, No. 183, dated July 7, 1863; No. 186, dated July 10, 1863; No. 190, dated July 14, 1863; No. 227, dated August 21, 1863; No. 230, dated August 24, 1863; No. 240, dated September 3, 1863, and No. 247, dated September 10, 1863, Headquarters, Department of the Missouri, Saint Louis, Missouri, and of which Colonel WILLIAM A. BARSTOW, 3d Wisconsin Cavalry, is President, were arraigned and tried—

1. *James R. Kirby*, citizen.

CHARGE I.—"Violation of the oath of allegiance."

Specification—"In this; that he, *James R. Kirby*, did, in or about the month of September, 1862, take and subscribe the oath of allegiance to the United States government, before an officer duly empowered and authorized to administer the same, by the terms of which said oath, he, the said James R. Kirby, bound and obligated himself to support, protect and defend the Constitution and Government of the United States, and bear true faith, allegiance and loyalty to the same; and afterwards, in or about the month of May, A. D., 1863, he, the said James R. Kirby, did violate his said oath of allegiance by accepting from the military authorities of the so-called Confederate States of America a commission to recruit for the army of the so-called Confederate States, and by attempting to raise and recruit men for service in the said so-called Confederate States army. This within the lines of the military forces of the United States, in the State of Missouri, in the year A. D., 1863."

CHARGE II.—"Violating the laws and customs of war."

Specification—"In this; that he, *James R. Kirby*, a citizen of Howard county, Missouri, did, in or about the month of May, A. D., 1863, in the State of Missouri, and within the lines of the regularly authorized and organized military forces of the United States, engage in enlisting and attempt to enlist recruits for service in the army of the so-called Confederate States of America, having received and accepted pretended authority so to do from the military authorities of the said so-called Confederate States of America. This in the State of Missouri, in the year A. D., 1863."

To which charges and specifications the accused, *James R. Kirby*, citizen, pleaded "Guilty."

FINDING.

The Commission having maturely considered the evidence adduced, finds the accused, *James R. Kirby*, citizen, as follows:—

CHARGE I.

Of the *Specification*, "Guilty."
Of the CHARGE, "Guilty."

CHARGE II.

Of the *Specification*, "Guilty."
Of the CHARGE, "Guilty."

SENTENCE.

And the Commission does therefore sentence him, *James R. Kirby*, citizen, "*To be shot to death, at such time and place as the Major-General commanding the Department may direct; two-thirds of the members of the Commission concurring in the sentence.*"

---

2. *Muse Kirby*, citizen.

CHARGE.—"Violation of the oath of allegiance to the United States government.

Specification—"In this; that he, *Muse Kirby*, did, in or about the month of September, A. D., 1862, take and subscribe the oath of allegiance to the United States government before an officer duly authorized and empowered to administer the same, by the terms of which said oath, he, the said *Muse Kirby* bound and obligated himself to support, protect and defend the Constitution and Government of the United States, and bear true faith, allegiance and loyalty to the same; and afterwards, in or about the month of October, A. D., 1862, he, the said *Muse Kirby*, violated his said oath of allegiance by joining and belonging to the company of one Hicks, Preston's regiment, outlaws, insurgents and guerrillas, rebel enemies of the United States, and by consorting with said company and regiment, and by unlawfully resisting and taking up arms against the lawfully constituted authorities of the United States, as an outlaw, insurgent and guerrilla and a rebel enemy of the United States, in the battle of Hartsville. This in the State of Missouri, in the years A. D., 1862 and 1863."

To which charge and specification the accused, *Muse Kirby*, citizen, pleaded "Guilty."

FINDING.

The Commission having maturely considered the evidence adduced, finds the accused, *Muse Kirby*, citizen, as follows:—

Of the *Specification*, "Guilty."
Of the CHARGE, "Guilty."

SENTENCE.

And the Commission does therefore sentence him, *Muse Kirby*, citizen, "*To be shot to death, at such time and place as the Commanding General of the Department may direct; two-thirds of the members concurring in the sentence.*"

---

3. *W. G. Watkins*, a captain of the army of the so-called Confederate States of America.

CHARGE.—"Violating the laws and customs of war."

Specification—"In this; that he, *W. G. Watkins*, a captain in the army of the so-called Confederate States of America, and an armed rebel against the authority of the Government of the United States, on or about the 28th day of January, A. D., 1863, was found in arms in the county of Saline, and State of Missouri, and within the lines of the regularly authorized and organized forces of the United States, having in his possession and on his person commissions and pretended authority to recruit for the armies of the said so-called Confederate States, of which commissions the following are copies:—

CAMP HINDMAN, MISSOURI,
September, 9, 1862.

'Captain W. G. Watkins is hereby authorized to recruit a company of cavalry, for the term of during the war, to consist of eighty able-bodied and well-mounted men, to furnish transportation and subsistence for the same, and to report to these headquarters whenever required.

(Signed,) J. V. COCKRELL,
'*Colonel Commanding, C. S. A.*'

'HEADQUARTERS, JACKMAN'S PARTIZAN,
'*November* 24, 1862.

'Captain WATKINS—

'SIR: In pursuance of an order from Major-General Hindman, commanding the Trans-Mississippi District, and Colonel Waldo R. Johnson, recruiting officer for the State of Missouri, you are hereby authorized to enlist and swear into the service of the Confederate States, for three years or the war, one company of men to serve as cavalry, and to compose a part of my independent regiment, now being raised to operate in the State of Missouri, and to report to these headquarters as soon as practicable.

(Signed,) S. D. JACKMAN,
'*Colonel Commanding.*'

He, the said Captain *W. G. Watkins*, having come within the lines of the said military forces of the United States, with the purpose and object of raising and recruiting men for service in the armies of the said so-called Confederate States. This in the State of Missouri, in the year A. D., 1863."

To which charge and specification the accused, *W. G. Watkins*, a captain of the army of the so-called Confederate States of America, pleaded "Not Guilty."

FINDING.

The Commission having maturely considered the evidence adduced, finds the accused, *W. G. Watkins*, a captain of the army of the so-called Confederate States of America, as follows:—

Of the *Specification*, "Guilty."
Of the CHARGE, "Guilty."

SENTENCE.

And the Commission does therefore sentence him, the said *William G. Watkins*, "*To be shot to death, at such place and time as the General Commanding the Department may direct; two-thirds of the members of the Commission concurring therein.*"

III...The proceedings, findings, and sentences of the Commission in the above cases of *James R. Kirby*, *Muse Kirby*, and *William G. Watkins*, were approved by the proper commanders, and the records forwarded for the action of the President of the United States.

The sentence in each case is approved, and will be carried out under orders of the army or department commander.

BY ORDER OF THE SECRETARY OF WAR:

E. D. TOWNSEND,

Assistant Adjutant General.

OFFICIAL:

Assistant Adjutant General.

Now that you have some idea of what occurred in the case of Muse Kirby we shall take a closer look at some of the trial details.

As stated at the start of this book, the procedure for a military court required that the court and its members be created for each defendant. During wartime, this was not an easy task. There were many officers to choose from, but there was also a heavy demand for their time and service.

In order to have some idea of what could and did happen on a frequent basis during the creation of a military court, read the orders on the following pages, which established the court that tried Muse Kirby:

Headquarters, Department of the Missouri.
St. Louis, Mo., July 7th, 1863.

SPECIAL ORDERS,
No. 183.

15.....A Military Commission is hereby appointed to meet at St. Louis, Mo., on Wednesday, the 8th inst., at 10 o'clock. A. M., or as soon thereafter as practicable, for the trial of such prisoners as may be brought before it.

DETAIL FOR THE COMMISSION.

Col. Wm. A. Barstow, 3d Wis. Cav.	Col. Albert Sigel, 5th Cav., M. S. M.
Lieut. Col. W. H. Stark, 24th Mo. Inf. Vols.	Maj. O. P. Newberry, 5th Cav. M. S. M.
Maj. H. M. Matthews, 3d Cav. M. S. M.	Capt. Chas. A. Meyer, Co. E, 1st Inf. M. S. M.

Maj. Allen Blacker, 1st Nebraska Vols., *Judge Advocate.*

No other officers than the above named can be assembled without manifest injury to the service.

By Command of MAJOR GENERAL SCHOFIELD.

J. A. CAMPBELL,
Assistant Adjutant General.

Headquarters, Department of the Missouri,
St. Louis, Mo., July 14th, 1863.

SPECIAL ORDERS,
No. 190.

5......Major O. P. Newberry, 5th Cavalry, M. S. M., is hereby relieved from duty as a member of the Military Commission of which Colonel Wm. A. Barstow is President. To date from July 10th, 1863.

By Command of MAJOR GENERAL SCHOFIELD.

J. A. CAMPBELL,
Assistant Adjutant General.

Headquarters, Department of the Missouri,
St. Louis, Mo., July 10th, 1863.

SPECIAL ORDERS,
No. 186.

6......Lieutenant Colonel Baumer, 1st Nebraska Infantry, is hereby detailed as a member of the General Court Martial and Military Commission convened by Paragraphs 14 and 15 of Special Orders, No. 183, from these Headquarters, and of which Colonel Barstow is President.

By Command of MAJOR GENERAL SCHOFIELD.

J. A. CAMPBELL,
Assistant Adjutant General.

Headquarters, Department of the Missouri,

St. Louis, Mo., Aug. 21st, 1863.

SPECIAL ORDERS,
No. 227.

14.—Captain EMIL STRADTMAN, 2d Missouri Artillery, will relieve Lieut. Col. BAUMER, 1st Nebraska Infantry, as a member of the Military Commission, of which Colonel W. A. BARSTOW, 3d Wisconsin Cavalry, is President.

BY COMMAND OF MAJOR GENERAL SCHOFIELD.

J. A. CAMPBELL,
Assistant Adjutant General.

Headquarters, Department of the Missouri,

St. Louis, Mo., Aug. 24th, 1863.

SPECIAL ORDERS,
No. 230.

6.—Capt. EDWARD E. ALLEN, Company "B," 31st Missouri Infantry Volunteers, will relieve Capt. CHAS. A. MEYER, 1st Infantry, M. S. M., as a member of the Military Commission, of which Col. BARSTOW is President, as soon as the Commission shall have disposed of the case now before it.

Upon being relieved, Capt MEYER will report for duty with his regiment.

BY COMMAND OF MAJOR GENERAL SCHOFIELD.

J. A. CAMPBELL,
Assistant Adjutant General.

Now that the court has been successfully established, we can move onto the trial details. We have already covered the charge and specification on Muse Kirby and we know he entered a plea of guilty. But what the short summation did not reveal was that once again, after the defendant entered a plea of guilty, he presented some facts to the court to help his case.

In the case of Muse Kirby, the first addition to the trial record was a statement made by Kirby that was to be given to the trial board. It appears that Kirby was not literate and a Union Army officer recorded his statement. The statement was as follows:

Statement of Muse Kirby, a prisoner at the Myrtle Street Prison, St. Louis, made on the 21st day of March, 1863. My age is eighteen years. I live in Stoddard County, Missouri. I was born in South Carolina. I was captured in Dunklin County on or about the fifth day of March, 1863. The cause of my capture, I was in rebel service. I was in arms against the United States and was a (rank) private in Hicks Company, Preston's Regiment. I was sworn into the rebel service about the fifteenth day of October, 1862 by Hicks in Stoddard County, Missouri for three years, or during the war. When captured, I was first taken to Bloomfield and remained there that night and was not examined then and was sent to Myrtle Street Prison about the seventh day of March, 1862. I took the oath of allegiance to the United States about the fifteenth day of September, 1862 before Captain Hyde at Bloomfield.

/s/ X (Muse Kirby's mark)

Subscribed by the prisoner the day first named in my presence,

/s/ L. A. Crane,

Lt., 14th Iowa Infantry.

The second addition to the trial record was a written interview that Kirby had taken part in when he was first captured. Kirby had answered a series of questions put to him by a Union Army officer. His answers were revealing and present us with a brief sketch of his life and military service.

The document reads as follows:

The prisoner makes additional statements as follows in answer to questions:

Q: How many times have you been in arms during the rebellion?

A: Twice

Q: What commanders have you served under?

A: Jeff Thompson and Preston.

Q: What battles or skirmishes have you been in?

A: Hartsville

Q: Did you have arms, or were you out on picket, or what part did you take in the action?

A: I had arms, and was in action with the rest.

Q: Have you ever furnished arms or ammunition, horse, provisions, or any kind of supplies to any rebels? State when, where, and how often.

A: No, Sir.

[The next question was a blank line, nothing was recorded]

Q: Have you ever been with anyone taking or possessing horses, arms or other property?

A: Have been with the company when they took some horses.

Q: Are you enrolled in the E. M. M., loyal or disloyal?

A: No, Sir.

Q: Are you a southern sympathizer?

A: No, Sir.

Q: Do you sincerely desire to have the southern people put down in this war, and the authority of the U.S. Government over them restored?

A: No, Sir.

Q: How many slaves have you?

A: None.

Q: Have you a wife? How many children?

A: Single.

Q: What is your occupation?

A: Farmer.

Q: What relations have you in the rebellion?

A: Three brothers.

Q: Have you ever been in any rebel camp? If so whose, where, and how long? What did you do? Did you leave it, or were you captured in it?

A: I was in the rebel service about three months with Thompson and about four months with Preston, was with Thompson before I took the oath. I know Ruben Harper when I see him. I don't know anything about his going south. He was arrested when I was. Don't think he belongs to the service. I want to be paroled if possible. If not, I wish to be exchanged.

/s/ X (Muse Kirby's mark)

Subscribed before me March 21st, 1863.

/s/ L. A. Crane,

Lt., 14th Iowa Volunteers.

Having entered a plea of guilty to the charge, and having added statements to hopefully cancel his death sentence, we have now reached the point were the trial record was sent to higher military authority for review. The Commanding General of the Department of Missouri, General John Schofield sent the transcript to Washington, D.C., with a recommendation that "punishment be commuted to imprisonment during the war."

The next step was a review of the case by the Judge Advocate General of the United States, Joseph Holt. On October 30, 1863, Judge Holt submitted the following summation to President Abraham Lincoln:

The within named Muse Kirby was charged with violating his oath of allegiance to the United States Government. Specification in that in September 1862, he took and subscribed to the oath of allegiance and afterwards in October joined a regiment of outlaws, insurgents, and guerrillas, consorted with them and took up arms against, and resisted the lawful authorities of the United States.

The prisoner plead guilty and offered no testimony or statement to the court. He was sentenced to be shot. General Schofield submits the case for the action of the President recommending that the sentence be commuted to imprisonment during the war.

Upon what grounds the recommendation was based does not appear. None are stated and the record furnishes none whatsoever. By admission of the prisoner to the Provost Marshal, immediately after his capture and which was accompanied with defiant expressions of hostility, it appears that he was in the rebel service under Jeff Thompson's command prior to October 1862. That after serving three months he left it, and took the oath of allegiance to the United States and in one month afterwards violated it and joined a company of rebels under one Hicks—fought against the government he had sworn to serve and uphold, and robbed and plundered those people who remained steadfast in their loyalty and fidelity. A more aggravated case of crimes confessed has seldom been brought before a military court, for no doubt is entertained that he took the oath with the intent and purpose to violate it on the first opportunity, and that he affected his purpose and intentions immediately and fully.

The loyal citizens of the State of Missouri have suffered unprecedented outrages from such bands of outlaws and guerrillas as the prisoner before us has acted with and as a measure of justice to the citizens as well as a military necessity, it is believed that exemplary punishment when ordered as in this case by a proper tribunal, should be summarily enforced.

The case then went to President Abraham Lincoln for the final decision. We can only speculate as to the turmoil it may have created for Lincoln. After all, his chief military advisor on the scene in Missouri recommended the death sentence be commuted to time in prison for the rest of the war. His chief legal advisor in Washington, D.C. presented the view that Kirby was a nasty, bad rebel outlaw, and should be shot to death.

On August 9, 1864, Lincoln made his decision. Once again, it was brief but very final. Lincoln wrote:

Sentence approved.
A. Lincoln

itary necessity it is believed
that exemplary punishment
when ordered as in this
case by a proper tribunal,
should be summarily
enforced.

Judge Advocate General.

Sentence approved
A. Lincoln
August 9, 1864

PRESIDENT LINCOLN'S SIGNATURE IN THE CASE OF MUSE KIRBY SENT THE YOUNG MAN BEFORE A FIRING SQUAD.

Chapter 10

The Gent Was a Spy

The next case concerns a violation of the laws of war, or, in simple words, the suspect was a spy. The trial takes place in the Southwestern District of the State of Missouri, specifically in Greene County, Missouri. The alleged objectives of the spy were the numerous Union Army forts and fortifications around the city of Springfield, Missouri.

The special order that created the military commission in this case was issued on August 28, 1862. The order contained the phrase we have already seen concerning the trial of "such other prisoners as may be brought before the court." In this military commission, the court members were a busy bunch of Union Army officers. The spy case in question was first brought before the court on October 29, 1862, the fifty-second day the commission was in service.

The suspect was named Charles H. Clifford. The charge was a violation of the laws of war. The first specification was as follows:

> *In this, that the said Charles H. Clifford, having joined and given in his adhesion [Author's note: They used the word adhesion] to the so-called Confederate States of America, in violation of his duties and obligations as a citizen of the United States, and having entered into the military service of the of the so-called Confederate States, and having received and accepted a commission as Major in the armies of the said Confederate States, now in open rebellion against the United States and engaged in carrying on active hostilities against the government and the authorities thereof, clandestinely, stealthily, and in disguise, and in the garb of a citizen, did leave the camps of the said rebel enemies of the United States,*

> *and pass within the limits of the military forces of the United States, in the Southwestern District of the state of Missouri, without any badge or mark designating his rank and without disclosing to the said military authorities his position or rank in the rebel armies, and with the intent and purpose of deceiving and evading the said military authorities and passing the military lines of said authorities in disguise, and without their knowledge and consent, contrary to the laws of war. This in Greene County, in the State of Missouri, on the twenty-first day of October, 1862.*

Specification number two was the same for the first several sentences and then went on a new track as follows:

> *...and garb of a private citizen of the United States, was found lurking about and near the fortifications of the post of Springfield, then and there being a military post of great importance in the Southwestern District of the state of Missouri, held by the military forces of the United States, and within the lines of the said Southwestern District of the State of Missouri; contrary to the laws and usages of war. This in Greene County, in the State of Missouri on the twenty-first day of October, 1862.*

Specification number three followed the same outline of facts as did the first two specifications and then went off onto another violation.

Number three stated:

> *...within the lines of the said Southwestern District of Missouri, and was arrested by the authorities of the United States, attempting in disguise as aforesaid, to escape from within the military lines of the said Southwestern District of Missouri, and from the said Post of Springfield for the purpose and with the intent of returning to the camps of the rebel enemies of the United States, contrary to the laws, and customs of war. This in Greene County, in the State of Missouri on the twenty-first day of October, 1862.*

The prisoner entered a plea of not guilty to all charges and specifications. The commission proceeded to the trial of Charles H. Clifford and the first witness was called to the stand. The following questions are by the Judge Advocate:

Q: What is your name, age, occupation, and place of residence?

A: My name is Robert P. Matthews. I am twenty-five years of age. I reside in Greene County in the state of Missouri. I am Captain of Company D, Eighth Regiment of Cavalry, Missouri Volunteers. My command is stationed at the present time at Springfield in Missouri.

Q: Are you acquainted with the prisoner at the bar, Charles H. Clifford, and if so how long have you known him?

A: I am not personally acquainted with him. The first time I ever saw him was on the evening of the twenty-first of this month.

Q: Where did you see him at that time?

A: I saw him on the roof of the residence of Colonel Boyd, near Springfield in this county.

Q: State to the court the circumstances of your visit to the residence of Colonel Boyd, the object of your visit, and what transpired there.

A: I was ordered by Lieutenant Colonel Baldwin of the Eighth Missouri Volunteers to take five men, and go and search the house and premises of Colonel Marcus Boyd to capture and bring into camp Major Clifford, if found there. I took Lieutenant Gibson and five men and repaired to the residence of Colonel Boyd. The sun was about one hour high when we left camp and we went out on the double-quick, and surrounded the house, some going up in front and some galloping around on the eastern side of the house to prevent anyone from escaping in that direction. We dismounted and entered the enclosure when one of my men, Private Capelt, called to me that he was on the house, being on the ell part and I could not be seen from the front. I passed around to the rear, and found him on the roof but he had already surrendered. He then passed back through a window into the front part of the building in the upper story. I then went around in the front of the house and the guard that went upstairs brought him down into the lower room. This was nearly at sunset. The sun still being a few minutes high. Major Clifford then demanded of me who I was sent to arrest and who I supposed I had arrested. I informed him I was sent to arrest Major Clifford. He said he was the man. He then insisted that I should take his parole to report at town. This I refused to do. He then asked for the privilege to change shirts, which I granted, and permitted him to return to his room under guard. When he came down I observed that he had also changed his pantaloons. When he was arrested, he had on a pair of blue federal uniform pantaloons. Those he had taken off, and put on a pair of dark colored pants. By that time a horse was brought out and we brought him to Colonel Baldwin's headquarters, and from there brought him into town.

Q: Did you see any other articles of Federal Uniform about his person?

A: I did not.

Q: Who did you find at the residence of Colonel Boyd at the time you made this arrest?

A: Mrs. Boyd, and a son of Colonel Boyd's. Mrs. Clifford, and the children, and servants, and another man who I did not know.

Q: What character did Major Clifford assume in conversation with you?

A: He told me in our conversation that he was an officer in the southern army.

Q: What rank did he assume to hold in the southern army?

A: He did not tell me his rank; he was called Major, and when he asked me to parole him, he placed his hand on his heart and said he would give me the word of a southern officer.

Q: How did the family act when you went there to arrest Clifford?

A: Mrs. Boyd and the female part of the family acted very rudely. Young Mr. Boyd acted like a gentleman. Mrs. Boyd was greatly excited and used very harsh language calling myself, and them that were with me, black republican sons-of-bitches. We made no reply, as it was not our business to do anything but arrest Mr. Clifford. She was in a great rage, and used a good deal of harsh language.

Q: Was anything said by those parties about the failure of Clifford to escape or leave?

A: There was a great deal said by the women during the time Clifford was on the house, but I did not pay any attention to anything that was said by them unless a pointed remark was addressed by them to me. My business simply being to secure Mr. Clifford.

Q: Was the rage manifested by those females the result of any improper conduct, or language on the part of you or your men, or whether it was simply the result of the capture of Clifford?

A: It was, I presume, the result of the capture, as my men acted throughout with entire propriety and decorum. I had ordered them to say nothing to the ladies improper and they obeyed the order.

Question by the Commission: Did Major Clifford make any remark while on his way to town (after his arrest) about his having been in our camps before?

A: I remarked to the Major on the way to town that he had come pretty close to our lines. He remarked that he had been closer than that, said he had been in a number of times, meaning as I understood him, that he had seen Colonel Boyd frequently. He also stated that he had run on our pickets some time previously. These statements were made in ordinary conversation, voluntarily.

Cross Examination by the Prisoner: When you first saw me, was I on the roof of the house or of the portico?

A: You was on the roof. I cannot say whether of the porch or the house, as they were under the same roof, you was in your sock feet, your boots being off.

Q: Did you consider me in a place of concealment?

A: I must confess that I thought you had just got out of bed, and had crawled out through the window with a view to make your escape to the brush near the farm.

Q: Do you think I could have jumped off that roof without danger of breaking my neck?

A: I think I would have risked the effort if I had wished to escape.

Q: Do you consider that I was in a place of concealment when you saw me?

A: I think not just then, for you was on the house, but seemed to have just come out of bed with the attempt to get to the brush.

The witness was excused from the stand and the next witness for the prosecution was brought to the stand and sworn to tell the truth. The witness testifies as follows:

Q: What is your age, name, occupation and place of residence?

A: My name is Joseph Cassell. I am twenty-one years of age, reside in Greene County, am a farmer, and at present I am a private soldier in Colonel Geiger's Eighth Missouri Cavalry Regiment of Volunteers.

Q: Are you acquainted with the prisoner, Major Clifford?

A: I know him; I never saw him until we arrested him.

Q: When did you arrest Major Clifford?

A: On the twenty-first of this month (October).

Q: Where did you arrest him?

A: At Colonel Boyd's.

Q: State the circumstances of the arrest.

A: We found him at Colonel Boyd's on the roof of the house; he had just come out on the roof. I drew my gun, and he said not to fire, he would surrender. I and another man went up through the house, opened the window, and took him, while the balance remained below.

Q: How was he dressed when you found him?

A: He had on a pair of blue soldier's pants, a dark colored shirt, and was bare-headed, and had no boots or shoes on. After we arrested him, and brought him downstairs he called for the Captain to come in. Mrs. Boyd told him there was no Captain there; one of the boys said there was a Captain there. She then ordered the door to be shut, saying she allowed no abolitionist to come inside of her house. The men then came in the house with the Captain. It was Captain Matthews. The prisoner then asked the Captain who he came to arrest, the Captain told him Major Clifford. The prisoner said he was the man, and asked for a parole 'til next morning. The Captain told him he had no authority to parole him. He then asked to change his clothes. The Captain permitted him to go to his room with a guard. I went as one of the guards. He changed his pants, and had a hat with cavalry sabers on it, these he pulled off of his hat, and threw them in the fireplace, and then we went down. He then asked me what regiment I belonged to. I told him I belonged to the Eighth Missouri. He said I was that much better off by it, for he did not know but that I belonged to the 'damned malish', about this time, Mrs. Boyd came up and wanted to know of me who reported the Major. I told her that I did not know anything about it. Mrs. Boyd then commenced talking to the Major. I do not remember precisely what the Major said, but Mrs. Boyd said the last one of us were 'damned fiends of hell.'

Q: What time of day did you arrest the prisoner?

A: I think the sun was about one hour or an hour and a half high, when we reached there, and left there just about sundown. I think they were on dress parade when we reached the camp.

Q: Did any conversation occur between the prisoner and any member of your party on the way to the camp?

A: I do not know; I was in the lead. Previous to leaving the house, he spoke to a little boy and pointing to the fireplace said something to him about a revolver, and told the boy to tell his wife to hide it. When we returned, the bricks were torn up, and misplaced but we did not find any revolver.

Question by the Commission: Was there a bed in the room where you arrested the prisoner?

A: Yes, Sir. Two of them.

Q: Had either of them the appearance of someone having left them?

A: Both of them looked as if someone had crawled from the both of them.

Cross Examination by the Prisoner: You said that the bricks were scattered in the evening when you went there the second time. In what condition were the bricks when you was there in the earlier part of the day? Were the bricks where they should have been in the fireplace, or were they torn up?

A: When we were there the first time, the bricks were piled up in the fireplace. When we returned there the second time, they were scattered.

Q: Did I throw the cross sabers behind the bricks in the fireplace, or did I put them on the mantelpiece over the fireplace?

A: You threw them then behind the piles of bricks that were in the fireplace. When we went back there, the cross sabers were on the mantelpiece.

Q: While waiting to change clothing, did you know the reason I was detained so long? If so, state the whole circumstances of my detention.

A: I know that you were waiting for your pants, there were several persons up there.

Q: While you was upstairs, how did I treat you — roughly or pleasantly? Either case, state the circumstances and the words spoken.

A: You treated me very well; offered me a chair to sit down. Your wife did the same.

Q: Did I show any disposition to attempt an escape?

A: No, Sir.

Q: When you first saw me, was I hidden?

A: When I first saw you, you was just getting out at the window. I cocked my gun and said 'there he is.' You said, 'don't fire, I surrender.'

Q: Do you know what the meaning of the word "funk" is?

A: I do not. I had never heard of the word before Mrs. Boyd used it.

Question by the Commission: Did the defendant give you any reason for wishing to change his clothes? If so, state it.

A: He said he had not changed his clothing since he came home. Mrs. Boyd said to him that he ought to wear the "feds" clothing. He said he came by them honest, if he had got them on. I understood the conversation to be about the pants.

Q: When you returned there in the evening did you find any pistol?

A: We did, under the head of his bed.

The witness was dismissed from the stand, and another person was called to testify on the part of the prosecution. The following questions are by the Judge Advocate.

Q: What is your name, age, occupation, and place of residence?

A: My name is Thomas A. B. Gibson. I am twenty-four years old. I live in Greene County, Missouri. I am a farmer and at present I am a Second Lieutenant in the Eighth Missouri Cavalry Volunteers."

Q: Are you acquainted with the prisoner, Mr. Clifford?

A: I am not acquainted with him; never saw him until we took him prisoner.

Q: When did you take him prisoner?

A: We took him prisoner on the twenty-first day of October, 1862. Captain Matthews was ordered to take five men; went out to Colonel Boyd's residence on a run. When we got there, I ran around on one side of the house, and the Captain on the other. We first saw the prisoner on the roof of the porch. The women came out in the yard where we were. I ran in and up the stairs, but could not get out that way. By this time, Clifford had got back in the house. We came down and asked Captain Matthews who he wanted. The Captain said Major Clifford. The prisoner said he was that man, and asked a parole 'til morning. Captain Matthews told him he had no authority to parole him, and that he would have to go with him to camp, and that he must get ready to go. During this time, the female members of the family, Mrs. Boyd in particular, appeared much incensed, and said she would protect her friends, and stand up and die by them. She said she had told Charlie that he had better run that we would catch him. She abused us very much; called us black republican sons of bitches, and black republican freaks of hell, and a thousand other abusive epithets. This was not in reply to anything said by the soldiers, for I heard none of them make any reply to the remarks.

Q: Did you come to town or to your camp in company of the prisoner?

A: I did.

Q: Did the prisoner disclose to you his rank or position, either at Colonel Boyd's or on the way to town?

A: He did, not only at the time of his arrest, but he said he was Major Clifford, an officer in the southern army and as such asked to be paroled until next morning.

Q: You say you was sent back to the place where the prisoner was found to examine the premises, and for other purposes. State what was the result of that further search.

A: I was ordered to go back and get a pair of federal pants which the prisoner had pulled off after we had arrested him. I reached Colonel Boyd's house perhaps at nine o'clock at night; told him I had been sent to search his house and asked him for a candle. He told me in a very gruff manor that he had no candles. I told him in a civil manner that I must have a candle, he told me 'God damn' me if I wanted a candle to go and get it. There was a piece of candle burning on the mantle. I took that, and with the men I had with me went upstairs, and there I found the federal uniform pants which Major Clifford had.

The court then adjourned for the day. The following morning, the fifty-third day the commission had been in session, the Judge Advocate sent a new witness to the stand to testify for the prosecution.

Q: What is your name, age, occupation, and place of residence?

A: My name is Marcus Boyd. My age is twenty-five years. I reside two and one half miles east of Springfield, Missouri. I am a farmer, and have been at my father's residence about two weeks.

Q: Are you acquainted with the prisoner Charles Clifford? If so, how long have you known him?

A: I am acquainted with him, and have known him three weeks, I suppose.

Q: Where did you first see the prisoner?

A: I first seen him in the state of Arkansas about fifteen miles north of Fayetteville.

Q: In what capacity did you find the prisoner acting there?

A: I first saw him in Colonel Coffee's camp of the confederate army. He seemed to have a good many acquaintances there. He came to me, and introduced himself to me, and appeared to belong to the army there.

Q: Did you learn from him what position of rank he held in the army there?

A: I cannot say that he told me himself; it was generally understood that he was a Major there, and he was called Major Clifford by those who held conversation with him in the camp.

Q: How long did you remain in Colonel Coffee's camp after forming the acquaintance of Major Clifford?

A: Two days; I formed his acquaintance on Saturday, and left Coffee's camp in company with him on Monday morning.

Q: In what direction did you travel after leaving Coffees camp?

A: We traveled from the camp of Coffee about fifteen miles north of Fayetteville to Harrisonville, and from Harrisonville to Carrolton, from Carrolton to Forsyth in this state, and from Forsyth to the residence of my father near Springfield.

Q: How far is it called from here to where Colonel Coffee was encamped at the time you and Major Clifford left his camp?

A: I believe it is called about one hundred miles.

Q: What was your object in traveling around by Harrisonville and Carrolton instead of coming by the direct route?

A: We wished to avoid capture on account of the federal soldiers there, also Colonel Coffee advised me to travel the route we came, and Major Clifford had some business on that route.

Q: About what time did you reach the residence of your father, Colonel Boyd?

The prisoner at this point asked the privilege of excluding witnesses from the courtroom who had given in their testimony. The courtroom was cleared for deliberation and after consideration of the subject the court overruled the motion.

A: About midnight, on Friday night having left Colonel Coffee's camp on Monday morning previous.

Q: How long did you remain in Colonel Coffee's camp?

A: I was there about one week.

Q: How was Major Clifford dressed on this journey?

A: He was dressed as a private citizen.

Q: Did you meet any federal troops on your journey at any place?

A: We did not. We did meet some provost guards in Arkansas who asked us for our passes. We showed them and they permitted us to pass.

Q: Did you keep the main road from Forsyth to your father's?

A: We did not; Jackson's, where we stayed at after leaving Forsyth, is not on the road from Springfield to Forsyth, we struck off from Jackson's and crossed Finley at Henderson's mill. There we struck across to the Rock Bridge Road, then we kept that road probably ten miles, then struck across to the old mine road, and came up that to my father's. My father lives about one half mile south of the Rolla road and outside of the pickets.

Q: Did you communicate the arrival of Major Clifford to anyone when you reached home?

A: To no one, only a Negro boy.

Q: When you reached home, what disposition did you and the Major make of yourselves?

A: I went to the kitchen and had a pallet made to sleep on, and remained there 'til daylight, and Major Clifford went to the barn.

Q: What precautions were taken to prevent the knowledge of Major Clifford's arrival from becoming public?

A: I took none myself, only to tell the Negro boy to not let my father know anything of it, the boy told me that my father had charged him to tell him if Clifford came about the premises at any time. I told him that he must not do it that; Clifford would soon be gone, and I would see that he should not suffer for failing to tell father. The children and Negroes, I presume, did not tell my father because they were instructed by my mother not to do so.

Q: Where had you been sojourning previous to visiting Coffee's camp?

A: I left home in August two years ago, and went to Pikes Peak, [Author's note: he refers to the mountain, Pikes Peak, in Colorado] thence to New Mexico. I left New Mexico for Texas about the last of March 1862, and remained in Texas 'til in July last, and then started north. I remained in Texas but a short time, and was sick all the while. In Texas, I avowed myself as a southern man.

Cross Examination by Prisoner: During our journey, did we travel through the woods or did we travel on public roads?

A: Generally, on public roads — except a short distance after leaving Forsyth, and during the time we traveled after night. I could not tell if the roads were public or not.

Q: Do you remember seeing a federal soldier in a house on the last day of our journey? If so, did I take any steps to avoid his vision?

A: I remember seeing a man dressed in federal clothing in a house that we passed. Major Clifford remarked that he belonged once to my brother's regiment.

Q: When we left Jackson's, do you know whether it would have been any further to your home the way which we came, than it would have been to have gone back and taken the main Springfield and Forsyth road?

A: I do not know; that was the first time I had traveled through that country.

Question by the Commission: You say you traveled on public roads; do you mean to say that you traveled on the public roads as roads most frequently used?

A: There may be other roads more traveled, but the roads we came seemed to be as much traveled as any others.

The Judge Advocate at this time announced that the evidence on the part of the prosecution was closed. The prisoner, Charles Clifford, was then duly notified of his privilege to introduce any evidence that he might desire. The prisoner here stated to the commission that he wished to prove by Mrs. Boyd, that the pants he was wearing when he was arrested were not worn by him for any purpose of disguise, but because the pants he wore to Colonel Boyd's needed washing, and change was made for that purpose.

Mrs. Boyd was called on the part of the defense, but not having taken the oath of allegiance, objection was made to admitting her as a witness. A General Order from the Commander of the Southwestern District of Missouri forbidding the commission to admit any witness before them who had not taken the oath. The Judge Advocate then offered to admit on the part of the prosecution the particular fact sought to be proved by this witness, and her testimony was waived by the prisoner. The prisoner, Charles Clifford, then announced that he had no other evidence to offer in his behalf and the evidence in the case was closed.

The prisoner, Charles Clifford, was then informed that he had the privilege of making any statement that he might desire in reference to the charges, the specifications, or the evidence adduced against him. The prisoner was granted time 'til tomorrow morning to prepare his statement.

Due to other matters, the prisoner was given an extra day to write his statement. The court met again on Saturday November 1, 1862. All members of the trial court on Major Clifford's case were present. Major Clifford, as part of his statement, told the court he was not guilty of the charge and set out to answer the specifications against him with a very long statement of the facts, as he saw them, relate to his defense. The statement of Major Clifford was as follows:

First, I deny being a 'citizen' of the United States of America when 'joining and giving in my adhesion' to the Confederate States of America. Secondly, I deny clandestinely, stealthily, and in disguise, leaving the encampment of the belligerent armies of the Confederate States, and passing within the limits of the military forces of the United States. Thirdly, I deny being found lurking in concealment about the fortifications of the Post of Springfield. Fourthly, I deny being arrested attempting to escape from the Post of Springfield to the camps of the belligerent armies of the Confederate States contrary to the laws, usages and customs of war, and call upon proof to the contrary very respectfully.

No evidence being brought to sustain the portion of the first portion of the first specification, specifically, that the said

Charles H. Clifford, having joined and giving in his adhesion to the so-called Confederate States of America in violation of his duties and obligations as a citizen of the United States and having entered the military service of the so-called Confederate States and having received and accepted a commission as a Major in the armies of the said Confederate States.

From this, I infer that no steps are taken to convict me on this point. On the second point, I deny clandestinely, stealthily, and in disguise leaving the encampments of the belligerent armies of the Confederate States, and passing within the limits of the United States Army.

To sustain this point, Mr. Marcus Boyd Jr. was called upon the stand, who is a Union man, and stated as follows, that we left the camp of Colonel Coffee fifteen miles north of Fayetteville on Monday morning, traveling east toward Marionville distant about twenty five miles from thence to Carrolton, then to Forsyth, from there to his home at his father's two miles and a half east of Springfield, arriving there about midnight on Friday. Upon cross examination, he stated on our way hither we traveled all the way on public roads, and that I took no steps to disguise myself or to avoid the vision of the public. He also stated that we passed a federal soldier, and that I took no steps to avoid him seeing me, and that I made some remark about him being a member of his brothers' regiment.

From the manner he describes our journey, he proves that we traveled in no haste. He was asked the reason why we did not come the nearest road from the camps to Springfield. To which he replied that he was sick, and did not wish to be stopped by the United States forces, who he understood to be then at Cassville. Furthermore, the witness stated that I had some business on the road which we did come. During the examination, the prosecuting party asked if he knew the reason for my coming, to which he replied that I had told him my object was to come to take out my wife, his sister, and residing at her and his father's two miles and a half east of Springfield, at which place I was made a prisoner by the Federal forces. He stated that upon our arrival there he did not know of any steps that I had taken to conceal my being there. He says that he saw me at the house soon after our arrival, and that he did not wish me to enter for fear that I would awake his father. He said that he had a conversation with a Negro who told him that Colonel Boyd (the father of the witness) had expressly commanded him (the Negro) to inform him (Colonel Boyd) if ever I should make my appearance there. The witness told the Negro not to tell Mr. Boyd of my being there; that he would be responsible that the Negro should sustain no injury by not informing Mr. Boyd of my being there. From this, the honorable members of the commission will see that had the journey hither been one of importance to the Confederate armies that I would have made haste on my journey.

The distance traveled by us was about 141 miles, at current traveling it could have been done within three days. Instead of this, we took five days and part of one night, to travel this distance. The witness stated I took no means to disguise myself, he said that I was dressed in clothing such as is worn by citizens, that I wore no uniform badges or marks of distinction. He also stated that we traveled public roads; in fact, as public as any in that part of the country, that we took no means to avoid the vision of any who might be on the roads or in houses by the roadsides, not only that, but he states we saw a Federal soldier on the road, and instead of trying to avoid him, I passed by and in passing made a remark that I knew him to belong to his brother's regiment. The gentlemen of the commission in all probability aware of the fact that the troops, both officers and soldiers of the Trans-Mississippi District wear no badge mark or uniform to distinguish them from citizens. If they do not, I will upon here state that they wear neither uniform badge or mark to indicate the officer or soldier. To prove this, permit me to call the attention of the gentlemen of the commission to the circumstances of my coming to the Post of Springfield. During the month of July 1862, with a flag of truce in an official capacity to exchange prisoners, you will find upon inquiring about the city of Springfield that I wore no uniform badge or mark, but that I was dressed as a citizen. Yet without uniform badge or mark, I was by General Brown recognized as a Confederate officer, and all of his communications to me were addressed as Major C.S.A. From the above I argue that my coming dressed as a citizen was in no manner or way in disguise.

From the circumstances of my intending to enter the house immediately upon my arrival proves that I did not seem anxious to conceal the fact of my arrival there. This is more apparent from the fact that the witness stated that the house was so full of strangers that even he had to sleep in the kitchen for want of a room in the house. His not wishing me to awaken his father proves that he was anxious either for the comfort of his father's luxury or else he did not wish his father to know of my being there. He may have had both of these motives in view, but in no way does this statement show any motive or any steps taken to conceal the fact of my being there at that time. No evidence has been produced to prove a single or solitary act which can be construed in such a manner which can convict or implicate me of trying in any way or manner to conceal my coming or being there at the residence of my wife. Neither on the road or at the house after my arrival. If anyone else or any other person, as an example Marcus Boyd Jr., should have taken any pains to try to conceal my having arrived there contrary to my knowledge or wish, I do not consider that I have responsibility for such action of other persons.

The evidence of Captain Matthews and Lieutenant Gibson merely describe the manner of my arrest upon which I have no comments to make any more than this to wit: That I was captured honorably they also prove that after my arrest I behaved myself as an officer and a gentlemen. As an officer, I knew I was entitled to a parole of honor, and upon this ground I asked Captain Matthews to accept it until the morning or, if he preferred it, I would report myself at any place that he would designate that evening. My reason for asking this parole according to the statement of the Captain was that I wished to exchange my clothing. He furthermore states that I said if he did not wish to accept my parole that if he would leave a guard with me I would come with the guard as soon as I could get ready. All of these propositions I made with my hand upon my heart in token of truth, avowing myself to be the one namely Major Clifford of the C.S.A. whom he had been sent to arrest. The Captain replied that his orders were strict, and that he could grant none of the propositions. I then asked him to send a guard with me to another room for the purpose of changing clothing which he did, on the road to the encampment of the command of which he was a member, a conversation occurred in which the Captain said something about my coming very near their encampment (distant about three-quarters of a mile) the exact words of my reply neither Captain Matthews or Lieutenant Gibson remembers, but it amounts to the fact I had said that I had been nearer Federal encampments than this, meaning the distance between the house of Colonel Boyd, and their encampment according to the Captain's construct.

They also (Captain Matthews and Lieutenant Gibson) state that I related an anecdote in connection with the above reply about my being on a scout, and coming in contact with Federal pickets, and how by hard running, according to the phrase used by the Captain, I escaped the pickets. The above reply I do not disown or deny, but make it good by saying that I have been nearer Federal encampments than I was at the time of my arrest, for explanation I will refer the honorable members of the commission to the narrative related by me to Captain Matthews, also the one which I told to some of the members of the commission on yesterday during recess from duty other circumstances I could relate, but do not think it all necessary, for I do think that not one of the honorable members of the commission, but is satisfied of the fact that I did not have any reference to my having been nearer to the Federal encampments during the interval of my arrival at the residence of my wife, and the time of my arrest. In fact, the words of my reply to the Captain in themselves show that I had no reference to the encampment of this command, nor do I see how my reply can in any way be construed so as to imply that I had taken any advantage of my manner to prove of any closer or of having been any nearer.

To the evidence of Joseph Cassell, I have to say that there were two errors in his evidence. He states that when he first saw me, I was coming through a second story window to the roof of a portico. This is false for he did not see me come through the window nor did he see me until, by coughing, I attracted his attention of my being there. He then stated I threw up my hands and said don't fire; I surrender. The expression made by me when he aimed his gun or musket at me was, I surrender. I did not say don't fire; don't fire. He then stated he was sent by the Captain to guard me while changing clothing. He stated that while there, I tore off a set of cross sabers from my hat, and threw them behind some bricks in the fire place which bricks were loose, and filled up in the fireplace. A part of this is also false, it is true that I did disengage a set of cross sabers from off of my hat in his presence, but so far from throwing them behind the bricks in the fireplace, I put them by the side of a pasteboard box on top of the mantelpiece over and above the fireplace, from the statement of the witness the honorable members of the commission, would perhaps think it was an act to conceal the cross sabers, but when you take in consideration, that I, in his presence without trying to conceal the act of my disen-

gaging the cross sabers, did do the act, then where is the act of concealment, after having done so without concealment or any act on my part trying to evade him seeing me, why then should I try to conceal them?

He further stated that on a subsequent visit to the house the cross sabers were found on the bricks in an exposed place to view, which bricks were not in the same state piled high in the fireplace as they were at the first time of his visit, but were strewn over the hearth. Whether this is true or not I do not know, if true I think that while moving the bricks in the fireplace the mantelpiece may have been shook hard enough to cause the cross sabers to fall from the mantelpiece, either between the wall and the mantelpiece, or they may have fallen off in front of this. I am not the Judge, but certain it is, and upon my honor as an officer and a gentlemen, I state, and with truth, that I did place the cross sabers on the mantelpiece above the fireplace. I also denounce and deny any intention of trying to conceal them; it seems very plain to me the witness had studied the portion of evidence which he gave against me for if he had not how could he have so very minutely have remembered every circumstance against me, and totally have forgotten some portions of the transactions which took place at the house, and about which he remembered only very little, in fact nothing, of some very important points; the honorable gentlemen of the commission no doubt remember his forgetfulness as well as I do upon points which I asked of which he remembered very little.

I will now make my statement upon my honor the circumstances and motives of my coming. I had tendered my resignation as before stated to General McBride and during the time that I was awaiting the return of the original resignation from the war department at Richmond, I was released from duty, I took this occasion to travel through some portions of Arkansas, and heard from what I considered reliable sources the information that ladies who were within reach of the Federal authorities were compelled to take the oath of allegiance to the United States Government and as punishment upon those who did not take this oath they were kept in a guardhouse for some time and then sent to prison in the north somewhere, in Illinois, or Iowa, or Wisconsin. I did not learn exactly where. It is a known fact that my wife resides near enough to Springfield to be within reach of the forces and authorities stationed there. I will now ask the commission the question, that had any one of you a wife, one whom you dearly loved (which you all would do if you had as good-looking a one as I have) would you not be uneasy about her? Would you not risk very much to see her to learn and know the truth and if possible try to rescue her from such danger, if the danger did exist? I know that you will answer in your own hearts that you would. Now gentlemen, this was my awful condition among my other adventures I happened by chance to meet my brother-in-law Mr. Marcus Boyd Jr., who was a little sick. He made propositions to me, as I had nothing else to do that I would bear him company home. The reason that he made this request was that he might possibly become very sick on the road, and among strangers he did not think he would fare as well as if he had a friend with him. Well, my desire being to come and see my wife was very strong it took but very little persuasion on his part to entice me to accompany him; sure enough we did come. He has described our journey, so I need say no more about that except I am happy to inform the honorable commission that we arrived safely two miles east of Springfield. There I remained until the day, hour, and minute of my arrest. During my stay there at the residence of my wife, I did not leave the premises of Colonel Boyd. In fact, I did not go 30 steps from the house in any direction, nor did I hold any communication with anyone that knew anything about the Post of Springfield in a military view of the word; in fact, I saw no one but the members of the family. As for the cross sabers which I disengaged from my hat, I will state that I did not myself put them on my hat nor do I know who did put them there. But I suppose that it was done by some female member of the family.

It is now three minutes of ten, and I must close my defense.

Summary,

I, Charles H. Clifford, Major of the Confederate States Army, off duty awaiting the returned recognition of my resignation as such officer, do deny absolutely and most emphatically having violated any law, custom, or usage, civil, or military, depriving me of the right of parole In this, that having left the Confederate camp and coming to the residence of my wife on my own private business, whose residence not being within the guards of the Post of Springfield, but distance two and a half miles, and not in a position commanding a view of said post or fortification and not having performed any other business directly or indirectly or been at any other point, and having been then and there arrested by the military authorities of the said post of Springfield and placed in their military prison.

Now I therefore, Charles H. Clifford, Major Confederate States Army in harmony with the laws, customs, and usages of war, and in compliance with the cartel entered into between the respective, United States, and Confederate Armies for the parole and exchange of prisoners of war, demand my parole of honor as such officer of the Confederate Army.

The room was then cleared for deliberation, and after maturely considering the charge, and specifications, and all the evidence adduced the court do find the prisoner Charles H. Clifford as follows:

Of the first specification: Guilty.

Of the second specification: Guilty.

Of the third specification: Guilty.

Except as much as he is charged with coming within the lines of the military authorities in the garb and dress of a soldier of the United States Army,

Of the charge: Guilty.

The court, two-thirds of the members therefore concurring, do therefore sentence the prisoner Charles H. Clifford to be hung by the neck until he is dead, at such time and place as the commanding officer of the department may designate.

W. M. ALBIN,
Lt. Col. 4th Cavalry, Missouri State Militia, Judge Advocate
Wm. JACKSON,
Major, 3rd Cavalry, Missouri State Militia, President.

With the guilty verdict on record, the death sentence was forwarded up the military chain of command for review. A document included in the transcript makes it clear that the case was referred from the Provost Marshal's office in St. Louis, Missouri, to the Provost Marshall in Washington. The document has faded badly during the years of storage, but one sentence remains readable:

As is submitted, this case comes under the provisions of Section 5, Act of July 17, 1862, and accordingly forward to for the action of the President.

The next entry in the transcript was the usual memo from Joseph Holt, Judge Advocate General of the United States. Holt included a brief summary of the case as follows:

The accused being a Major in the Confederate Army in the disguise and dress of a citizen passed our military lines and was arrested at the house of a private citizen; he making a full confession of his identity. His conduct was unquestionably a grave offense against the laws and usages of war and deserves severe punishment. He is not charged in so many words with being a spy but the court probably so regarded him, and hence he was condemned to suffer death by hanging.

The disguise, which he assumed, strips him of all claims to be treated as a prisoner of war. The pretense urged in his defense that he had entered our lines for the purpose of seeing his wife was not supported by any proof.

On May 11, 1863, President Abraham Lincoln had the final word in this case.

Lincoln wrote:

> *Sentence commuted to confinement in one of the military prisons for during the war.*
> *A. Lincoln*

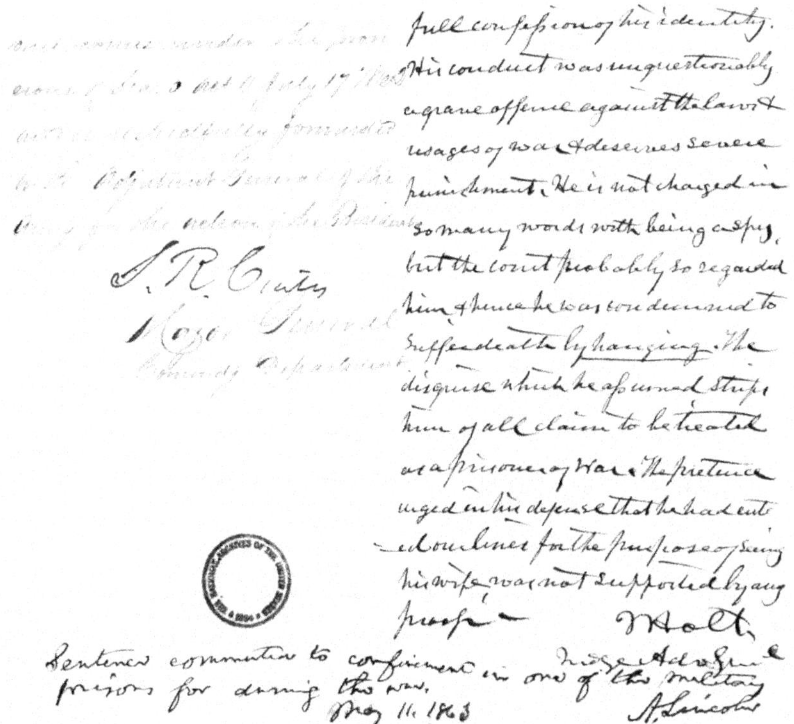

full confession of his identity. His conduct was unquestionably a grave offence against the laws & usages of war & deserves severe punishment. He is not charged in so many words with being a spy, but the court probably so regarded him & hence he was condemned to suffer death by hanging. The disguise which he assumed strips him of all claim to be treated as a prisoner of War. The pretence urged in his defense that he had entered our lines for the purpose of seeing his wife was not supported by any proof —

J Holt,
Judge Advocate General

S. R. Curtis
Major General
Commanding Department

Sentence commuted to confinement in one of the military prisons for during the war.
May 11. 1863
A. Lincoln

President Abraham Lincoln's final decision regarding the spy case on Major Charles H. Clifford, C.S.A.

Chapter 11

The Last Trial Chapter

In this last chapter, I've included a series of short trials. Actually, more of a summary like the one we found in the chapter on Muse Kirby. We have new charges unlike any in this book so far, and we have old charges with an odd ending. The entire idea is to present the American Civil War in such a way as to be very interesting, and with a high degree of entertainment. In my books, I try to present the material in such a way as to promote the enjoyment of history. I hope you do enjoy the variety of charges in this last chapter.

During my research for this book, I looked at a lot of Union Army trial cases. I could not help but get the feeling that these military courts were simply a rubber-stamp operation to eliminate opposition. You know the feeling — bring that next guilty rebel in here for his fair trial. And, surprise, the rebel was convicted on all charges. While there is little doubt that these military courts were very hard on the people unlucky enough to be brought before them, it would be unfair of me to call them a rubber-stamp operation. Just when you thought their only purpose in life was to be ruthless and crush all defendants, along comes a case of a very lucky rebel like Joseph Aubuchon.

GENERAL ORDERS No. 12.
HDQRS. WESTERN DEPARTMENT,
Saint Louis, Mo., September 16, 1861.

I. Before the military commission which convened at the Saint Louis Arsenal on the 5th instant, pursuant to Special Orders No. 118, current series, from these headquarters, was tried — Joseph Aubuchon.

CHARGE: Treason against the Government of the United States.

Specification: In this, that Joseph Aubuchon, of the town of Ironton, Iron County. State of Missouri, did assume an attitude of open rebellion against the Federal Government by taking up arms against the same, by assuming and exercising the functions and office of Lieutenant in the rebel army within the limits proper of the State of Missouri from and after about the twentieth day of August, 1861.

FINDING AND SENTENCE: The commission find the prisoner as follows:

Of the specification, guilty, except the words "By taking up arms against the same, by assuming and exercising the functions and office of Lieutenant in the rebel army."

Of the charge, guilty.

And does therefore sentence him, Joseph Aubuchon, to be confined at hard labor during the existing war and to have his property confiscated.

II. The proceedings, findings and sentence of the commission are approved.

On the recommendation of the members of the commission and in consideration of the fact, the offense charged occurred previous to the proclamation of the Commanding General of the Department, the sentence against Joseph Aubuchon is remitted. He will be released from confinement and permitted to return to his home.

By order of Major General Fremont:
J. C. KELTON,
Assistant Adjutant General

But only five days later, a second rebel enemy of the United States was charged and tried for treason against the United States. The first trial was held in St. Louis. This next trial was held at Ironton, Missouri. They did not quite turn out the same way.

SPECIAL ORDERS No. 2.

HEADQUARTERS,

Ironton, Mo., September 24, 1861.

Before the military commission, which convened at Ironton, Missouri, September 21, 1861, was tried:

William Perry.

CHARGE: Treason against the United States Government.

I. The commission in the case of William Perry finds him guilty of treason and sentence him to hard labor during the war, and all his real estate and personal property (if any there be) is hereby confiscated and declared the property of the United States.

II. The proceedings and finding of the commission in the case of William Perry are approved. Colonel Hovey, Thirty-third Illinois Volunteers, will see that the prisoner is kept at work on the fort at Ironton and that he is kept in charge of the guard when not at work. The commanding officer at Potosi will seize all personal property that may belong to said William Perry and forward it to the quartermaster at this post who will account for it to the United States and use it for the public service. The commanding officer at Potosi will also report if William Perry owns any real estate in or near Potosi.

By Order of Colonel Carlin, Commanding:

A. L. BAILHACHE,

Adjutant.

In a great many ways, the American Civil War set new standards for methods of warfare. For example, the Union Army was very good at using the great rivers of our land to military advantage. They developed a new type of gun-boat to fire on confederate forts along the rivers. They also created a series of hospital ships that operated on the Mississippi River to care for wounded soldiers. Thus, when there was an attack against the river forces, the Union Army took that as a serious affair.

At the military commission, which convened at Columbia, Missouri, pursuant to Special Orders No. 160, of February 20, 1862, from the headquarters Department of the Missouri, and of which Lt. Colonel William F. Shaffer, Regiment Merrill's House, is president, were arraigned and tried:

Calvin Sartain.

CHARGE: Violation of the laws of war by attacking a vessel transporting U.S. troops.

Specification 1: In this, that the said Calvin Sartain, a citizen of Howard County, Missouri, did shoot and discharge a loaded gun at and into the steamer White Cloud, which said steamer was being used for the transportation of troops of the United States on the Missouri River; and the said Sartain did thereby with malice aforethought kill and murder a certain person whose name is unknown, the pilot of said boat. This near the Missouri River in Howard County, Missouri on or about the twenty-fifth day of August 1861.

Specification 2: In this, that the said Calvin Sartain, a citizen of Howard County, Missouri did aid and abet certain persons whose names are unknown in an armed attack upon the steamer, White Cloud, which said steamer was engaged in the transportation of U.S. troops on the Missouri River. This near the Missouri River in Howard County, Missouri on or about the twenty-fifth day of August, 1861.

To which charge and specifications the prisoner pleaded not guilty.

The commission finds the prisoner as follows:

On the first specification, guilty, except as to the murder and killing of a certain person whose name is unknown, the pilot of the boat.

Of the second specification, guilty.

Of the charge, guilty.

And does therefore sentence him, Calvin Sartain, to be shot to death at such time and place as the commanding general of this department may direct.

Finding and sentence approved. Sentence will be carried into effect at a time and place to be hereafter designated by the general commanding this department. In the meantime, the prisoner will be confined in the military prison at Alton.

In the next case, we have once again a violation of the oath of allegiance. After looking at a number of these cases it seems that almost every court had a different view of the serious nature of the offense. In many cases the luck of the draw, or which court was assigned to your case, played a major part in the severity of your punishment. We have the case of A. W. Mires, a citizen of Mississippi County, Missouri on the following charge and specification. The charge was Violation of the Oath of Allegiance.

The specification was as follows:

In this, that he, A. W. Mires, a citizen of Mississippi County Missouri, on or about the sixth day of June 1862 at Hickman Kentucky, did take and subscribe the oath of allegiance to the government of the United States before an officer duly authorized and empowered to administer the same; by the terms of which said oath, he A. W. Mires, bound and obligated himself to support, protect and defend the Constitution and Government of the United States and bear true faith, allegiance and loyalty to the same: and afterward on or about the fifteenth day of December 1862 the said A. W. Mires did violate his said oath of allegiance by joining and belonging to Company E, Eighth Regiment of Missouri Cavalry Confederate States of America, rebel enemies and by consorting with said company and regiment and by resisting and taking up arms against the regularly organized and authorized forces of the United States as an insurgent, outlaw and rebel enemy.

Once again, the prisoner entered a plea of not guilty, and after mature deliberation, the court found him guilty on all charges:

And the commission does therefore sentence him, A. W. Mires, citizen, to be confined during the war at such place as the General Commanding the Department shall direct.

Finding and sentence confirmed. The sentence will be carried into effect at the Military Prison, at Alton, Illinois under the direction of the Provost Marshal General.

Exactly what is a charge of disloyalty? What do you have to do to be charged with this crime? The next case touches on this issue. In order to understand the intense feeling that could have been associated with this trial the reader needs a little background information. On Sept. 27, 1864, "Bloody Bill" Anderson, a feared confederate guerrilla leader in the northern part of Missouri, had ambushed the north-bound train from St. Louis, Missouri at the Centralia Railroad Station. Anderson and his men removed twenty-one unarmed Union Army men from the train and shot them. He also robbed the passengers and burned the train. The murder of the helpless Union soldiers produced an intense feeling of rage and anger within the Union Army in Missouri.

Thomas O'Neil, a citizen of the United States, on the following charge and specification.

The charge was disloyalty.

The specification: In this, that he, Thomas O'Neil, a citizen of the United States and owing allegiance thereto, on or about the third day of October A.D. 1864, in the city of St. Louis did say in the presence of D. W. Stedman, and a large number of other citizens that "I consider Bill Anderson did right in killing Union Soldiers at Centralia in Northeast Missouri, in the recent rebel raid there," or words to that effect, with other language of like import and tendency, he, the said Thomas O'Neil, thereby manifesting his disloyalty, and his sympathy with guerrillas, bushwhackers, and rebel enemies of the United States.

The prisoner entered a plea of not guilty to the charges, and the trial went forward. But in this case the verdict was a complete surprise, the court found him not guilty:

And the commission does therefore acquit him, Thomas O'Neil, citizen. Finding and acquittal confirmed.

The prisoner will be released from custody, on taking the oath of allegiance and giving bond in the sum of five hundred dollars with good and sufficient surety for his future good conduct as a loyal citizen, under the direction of the Provost Marshal General.

The next case sounds interesting. It may well have been a case where the full trial transcript should have been ordered. The violation of the oath of allegiance sounds routine, but charge number two with the reference to "did lurk and travel about" within the state sounds like some type of spy story. And so, we move onto the trial of Lafayette V. Hall, a citizen of Moniteau County, Missouri, on the following charges and specifications. The first charge was a violation of the oath of allegiance.

The specification reads as follows:

In this, that he, Lafayette V. Hall, did, in or about the month of January, 1862, at Moniteau County, Missouri, take and subscribe the oath of allegiance to the Government of the United States, by the terms of which said oath, he, the said Lafayette V. Hall, bound and obligated himself to support, protect and defend the Constitution and Government of the United States, and bear true faith, loyalty, and allegiance to the same; and afterward, on or about the fourth day of November, 1863, he, the said Lafayette V. Hall violated his said oath, by joining and belonging to Company D, Elliott's said Company and Battalion, and by resisting and taking up arms against the regularly authorized and organized authorities of the United States, as an outlaw, insurgent, and a rebel enemy. This, in the State of Missouri.

The second charge was listed as a Violation of the Laws of War. The specification read:

In this, that he, Lafayette V. Hall, a rebel enemy of the United States and a soldier of the army of the so-called Confederate States of America, did, in or about the month of August, 1864, enter and come within the lines of the military forces of the United States, and without ever having reported himself to any of the military authorities of the United States, or renewed his allegiance thereto, did lurk and travel about within the State of Missouri, until arrested in Moniteau County, Missouri, in or about the month of August, 1864.

The prisoner entered a plea of guilty to the first charge. However, he entered a not guilty plea to the second charge. Mr. Hall evidently felt that while he did join the rebel army he did not "lurk and travel about" in Missouri. After a trial, the Union Army officers on the court found him guilty on all counts.

And the Commission does therefore sentence him, Lafayette V. Hall, citizen, to be confined during the war, at such place, as the General Commanding the Department shall direct.

Finding and sentence confirmed. The sentence will be carried into effect at the Military Prison at Alton, Illinois, under the direction of the Provost Marshal General.

The next case might be unusual to our modern way of thinking. I will admit it even surprised me when I uncovered the information. Somehow it had never occurred to me that someone might want to steal a bale of cotton.

And now we have the trial of John Hanrahan, a citizen of the State of Missouri, on the following:

The charge: Larceny.

The specification: In this, that he, John Hanrahan, did, at Saint Louis, Missouri, on or about the twenty-eighth day of September, 1864, feloniously take, steal, and carry away, a quantity of cotton of the value of ten dollars, belonging to the Government of the United States, with intent to convert the same to his own use.

The prisoner entered a plea of not guilty, and after the trial the court announced to the world that he was, in fact, guilty.

And the Commission does therefore sentence him, John Hanrahan, a citizen, to be confined in the Penitentiary of the State of Missouri, at Jefferson City, Missouri, for the period of two years.

Finding and sentence confirmed. The sentence will be carried into effect under the direction of the Provost Marshal General.

The next case sounds like something we have already read about. In fact, it is a second case involving the theft of a bale of cotton from the Union Army. It sounds familiar because the location, date of theft, and value taken are the exact same as the case we just covered. It appears that Mr. Hanrahan may have had a partner in crime.

We move forward to the case of Matthew Price, a citizen of the State of Missouri, on the following charge and specification:

The charge: Larceny.

The specification: In this, that he, Matthew Price, did, at the City of Saint Louis, Missouri, on or about the twenty-eighth day of September, 1864, feloniously take, steal, and carry away, a quantity of cotton, of the value of ten dollars, belonging to the Government of the United States, with intent to convert the same to his own use.

Again, the prisoner said not guilty, and after the trial the trial commission said guilty.

And the Commission does therefore sentence him, Matthew Price, a citizen, to be confined in the State Penitentiary of the State of Missouri, at Jefferson City, Missouri, for the period of two years.

Finding and sentence confirmed. The sentence will be carried into effect under the direction of the Provost Marshal General.

At first glance, the next case seems to be unusual. But after you read and think about the charges for a minute, it makes sense that such a grouping of charges could occur.

We now cover the trial of Thomas Blalock, a citizen of Cooper County, Missouri, on the following charge and specifications:

The charge: Violation of the oath of allegiance to the United States.

The specification: In this, that he, Thomas Blalock, did, in or about the month of January, A.D.1862, take and subscribe the oath of allegiance to the Government of the United States, in the county of Cooper, State of Missouri, before an officer duly authorized and empowered to administer the same; by the terms of which said oath, he, the said Thomas Blalock, bound and obligated himself to protect, support and defend the Constitution and Government of the United States, and bear true faith, loyalty and allegiance to the same; and afterward, on or about the first day of July, A.D.1864, he, the said Thomas Blalock, violated his said oath by joining and belonging to the rebel army, and by resisting and taking up arms against the lawfully authorized and organized forces of the United States, as an outlaw, insurgent, and rebel enemy. This in the State of Missouri, A.D. 1864.

The second charge was larceny. The specification was:

In this, that he, Thomas Blalock, did, in or about the month of August, A.D. 1864, near the Osage River, in the State of Missouri, feloniously take, steal and carry away, from a person whose name is unknown, a bay mare, of the value of forty dollars, the lawful property of him, the said person whose name is unknown, with the intent and purpose of converting the said mare to his own use.

This in the State of Missouri, A.D. 1864.

In this case, the prisoner said he was not guilty of the violation of the oath of allegiance. But, he did admit to stealing the horse. Following a trial, the court found the defendant guilty on all counts.

And the Commission does therefore sentence him, Thomas Blalock, citizen, to be confined for the period of ten years, in the State Penitentiary of the State of Missouri, at Jefferson City, Missouri.

Finding and sentence confirmed. The sentence will be carried into effect under the direction of the Provost Marshal General.

Our final case of this chapter concerns a case of smuggling. Reading the details opens up many questions about wartime controls over some common-use items. It also makes one wonder about the system of business regulations the Union Army had in place during the war. We now move to the case of Jacob P. Weller, citizen of Lawrence County Arkansas, on the following charge and specification.

> *The charge: Smuggling.*
>
> *The specification: In this, that he, Jacob P. Weller, citizen, in or about the month of September, 1864, at St. Louis, Missouri, with intent and purpose of furnishing and supplying the rebel enemies of the United States with articles contraband of war, did bargain for and buy about twelve ounces of quinine, and various other articles, the sale of which was prohibited in the Department of the Missouri, and in the District of St. Louis, without a permit from the military authorities being first obtained, and in pursuance of his said purpose he, Jacob P. Weller, was in the act of so conveying and delivering said contraband articles to the rebel enemies of the United States, when arrested in New Madrid County, Missouri, in or about the month of September, A.D. 1864.*

As usual, the prisoner said, "not guilty," and after a trial the court said, "guilty."

> *And the Commission does therefore sentence him, Jacob P. Weller, citizen, to be fined in the sum of five hundred dollars, and to be imprisoned until the same is paid, provided that the term of said imprisonment does not exceed three years.*
>
> *Finding and sentence confirmed. The prisoner will be released from custody under the direction of the Provost Marshal General, upon payment of the fine to the Chief Quartermaster of the Department of Missouri.*

Bibliography

Most of the Missouri information for 1861 and 1862 that I used in this book can be found in the remarkable Civil War Historical Project undertaken by the U.S. Government after the Civil War. The official title is *The War of Rebellion, Official Records*. This work was designed as a series, with a total of one hundred twenty-eight books printed. If you desire to research American Civil War history, you'll need to become well-versed in this project — usually referred to as the *OR*. Most of the material for this book comes from *Series II*, which, in part, deals with prisoners of war. Thus, the correct cite for the bibliography would be: *The War of the Rebellion, Official Records, Series II, and Volume No*. If you can find a set of the *OR* that has the consecutive number system added, then you can also identify a book by its exact sequential number. Much of my reprinted material comes from book number 114.

I kept my bibliography simple. I cited the use as: *OR*, book number, and the page number on which the material can be found. In the case of the actual trial transcripts, a record group tells you where to find the cases created by specific groups, such as the Union Army. The folder number in question holds the entire transcript. For a fee, you may order a copy of the entire document from the National Archives and Record Administration.

Chapter 1:

Fremont Proclamation; *OR*, Book 114, pgs 221-222

General Orders No. 32; *OR*, Book 114, pg 237

Lincoln Suspend Habeas Corpus; *OR*, Book 114, pg 233

United States v. W. L. Tilley; *The Tilley Treasure* by James B. King, Jr., 1984, School of the Ozarks Press, pgs 104-145

General Orders No. 17; *OR*, Book 114, pgs 281-282

Price Proclamation; *OR*, Book 114, pgs 180-181

Thompson Proclamation; *OR*, Book 114, pg 181

Chapter 2:
COL Deitzler Trial Mistake; *OR*, Series I, Book 8, pgs 822-823
General Orders No. 1; *OR*, Book 114, pgs 247-249
Trial of William Combs; *OR*, Book 114, pgs 427-431
Trial of William Hearst; *OR*, Book 114, pgs 285-292

Chapter 3:
United States v. Francis Musgrave; National Archives Record Group 153, Folder #MM672

Chapter 4:
United States v. Pvt. Edward Eastman; National Archives Record Group 153, Folder #LL2601

Chapter 5:
United States v. Pvt. John Campbell; National Archives Record Group 153, Folder #MM954

Chapter 6:
Trial of Edmund J. Ellis, *OR*, Series II, Book 114, pgs 453-457

Chapter 7:
United States v. Pvt. Sherman Dodge; National Archives Record Group 153, Folder #MM937

Chapter 8:
United States v. Pvt. Jasper Laster; National Archives Record Group 153, Folder #MM1331

Chapter 9:
United States v. Muse Kirby; National Archives Record Group 153, Folder #MM1016

Chapter 10:
United States v. Charles H. Clifford; National Archives Record Group 153, Folder #MM128

Chapter 11:
Selected Short Cases from the National Archives Record Groups, et al.

Index

A

B

Meet The Author

My father was a WWII and Korea Veteran who retired from the U. S. Army after twenty-two years of service. Dad settled our family in Salem, Missouri, and as a result I'm a 1965 graduate of Salem Senior High School. I attended the School of the Ozarks at Pt. Lookout, Missouri and graduated with a bachelor's degree in Sociology in August of 1969. I entered the Missouri State Highway Patrol Academy immediately after college on September 16, 1969. Upon graduation from the MSHP Academy, I was assigned to the Waynesville/Ft. Wood Zone of Troop I in December of 1969. Pulaski County has been my home since then. My career with the Patrol resulted in many commendations, and I'm one of a very small group of Troopers who've been awarded the Medal of Valor by the Missouri State Highway Patrol. I retired as the Local Zone Sergeant in June of 2001. Shortly after retiring, I became a Reserve Officer for the Waynesville City Police.

In 2004, I ran for the elected office of Sheriff of Pulaski County. I won the first race, and I was re-elected for a second four-year term in 2008. The eight years I spent as Sheriff of Pulaski County presented me with more challenges and difficulty than I'd ever faced before. I retired as Sheriff on December 31, 2012. The following week I became a Deputy serving under our new sheriff. I'm currently assigned to the Detective Division as a Reserve Officer who specializes in cases of financial exploitation against older adults. In 2017, I'll start my 47th year in active law enforcement.

I'm married to the former Cheryl Ann Moore of Dixon, Missouri and I have one son, Taylor. I'm a life member of the NRA and a past president of the Old Stagecoach Stop Foundation.

I've written two books about the American Civil War in Missouri. These books are: *The Tilley Treasure*, and *Justice*. The Civil War in Missouri was vastly different from the Civil War that was fought in the southern and eastern states. Both books present the reader with a unique look at how the Civil War affected the border state of Missouri, as citizens struggled to live in a war-torn region. At present, I'm working on several more books based on history and my law enforcement career.

www.ingramcontent.com/pod-product-compliance
Lightning Source LLC
Chambersburg PA
CBHW071216090426
42736CB00014B/2848

* 9 7 8 1 9 4 3 2 6 7 3 2 3 *